Aurea Vidyā Collection*

——————— 12 ———————

*For a complete list of Titles, see page 163.

This book was originally published in Italian as, Raphael, *La Scienza dell'Amore*, by Edizioni Āśram Vidyā, Rome, Italy

First published in English in 2010 by Aurea Vidyā 39 West 88th Street, New York, N.Y. 10024, U.S.A. www.vidya-ashramvidyaorder.org

Set in font ©Vidyā 12/13 points by Aurea Vidyā

Printed and bound in the U.S.A.
by Lightning Source, La Vergne, TN, USA

ISBN   978-931406-12-3
Library of Congress Control Number: 2010900047

On the Cover: The Heliopolis Obelisk
                Central Park, New York, N.Y.

RAPHAEL
(Āśram Vidyā Order)

The Science of Love

From the desire of the senses
to the Intellect of Love

AUREA VIDYĀ

«The love that moves the sun and the other stars»

Dante

Paradiso, **XXXIII**, 145

TABLE OF CONTENTS

Foreword   11

Polar Systems   15

The Psycho-physical and Spiritual   23
  Constitution of the Entity

The Unity-Trinity of the Entity   33

The Conception of Love   41

Couples at Different Levels of Polarity   63

Polarity within the Human Organism   71

The Configuration of the Entity according   77
  To the Cakra

Eros in Greek Mythology   85

Platonic Eros   97

Love is Beauty   113

Glossary   135

Index   145

Raphael: Unity of Tradition   157

Please note

Many words along the text have been used in their Traditional meaning and, as this may differ from common usage (e.g. sensible), the reader is encouraged to refer to the Glossary on page 135, where also several definitions of Greek as well as Sanskrit words are given.

The excerpts from Dante's *Paradiso*, all along the text, are quoted from: Dante Alighieri, *The Divine Commedy, Part III, Paradise*. Translated by Dorothy L. Sayers and Barbara Reynolds. Penguin Books.

FOREWORD

To write about male-female polarity and about Love within the human dimension is no easy task, because of the complex manifestations of sex, emotion-sentiment, love and the spiritual aspect from which the Creature-Creator polarity emerges.

The problem is so vast that we must make it clear that we have barely touched on it here; however, we believe that we have provided a sufficiently thorough overview of the question to act as a guideline to those earnestly endeavouring to comprehend the phenomenon.

Naturally the following considerations are addressed above all to aspirants and disciples who have embarked upon the pathway of traditional "Philosophical Love". The reader is therefore presumed to have at least a basic knowledge of the problem and a strong yearning to practice that Love which neither disappoints nor causes pain or ambiguity, so as to be able to demonstrate to himself the validity of a path based on the "power" of Love.

In present-day culture the word "love" is unfortunately taken primarily to indicate sex, and, even when speaking of feelings, they are always qualified in terms of sexual elements. This happens to such an extent that personal identity is associated with sex, failing which the human being feels as if he were crumbling and at a loss for reference points.

Hence the actions of human beings, however much they may be spread over several fields, are always seen as fundamentally functional to the male-female polar sphere, rather than to the man-woman aspect or to that of the *person* having a body, a psyche and also a soul.

When, on the other hand, a culture eliminates the reality of the Soul from its heritage, it is obvious that all action is then directed towards its formal aspect; that is to say, towards the gross physical world. Therefore, in such a culture the human being is primarily a mere body which exudes thoughts, feelings and sexuality. By reducing human beings to such factors, which are clearly contingent and reductive, it follows that they find themselves in a condition of anxiety, frenetic quest without solution and fossilisation of the psyche to the point of producing that alienation which we witness.

In this book we have tried to present sexuality as a biological activity, the sphere of the affections as a psychological expression and, lastly, "Philosophical Love" as innate to the Soul representing one's supra-individual or supra-egoic center.

May these notes, although very brief, be a source of help to those who are upon the pathway of the Knowledge of Love as pure Universal Principle.

"But thy ascent, if rightly I compute,
Ought no more to surprise thee than to see
A stream rush down from mountain crest to foot;

Nay, but if thou, from every hindrance free,
Shouldst hug the ground, that would be a surprise
As stillness in quick flame on earth would be."

Then back again to heav'n she turned her eyes.

Paradiso, I, 136-142

POLAR SYSTEMS

«When a negative pole opens his
Heart to a positive pole, a flashing
of lightning explodes, and the space
savors the elation of Beauty»

Raphael

The Threefold Pathway of Fire, I, II, 4

1. When we speak of polarity we mean a factor which manifests itself upon all the planes of existence and which expresses itself in terms of positive and negative or receptive, of male and female, of active and passive functions, even of dynamic and static forces, etc. Every existential plane has its own peculiar polarities which are expressions of that particular state; thus upon the dense physical plane we have a series of polarities which are to be found in the atom, in electricity, in astronomy, at an organic level, etc.

Polarity, not being an absolute duality, presupposes a source of unity from which it stems.

2. Unity, by splitting, produces the two; the point, depolarizing, creates the line;

thus, Adam (positive polarity) becomes specific in Eve (negative polarity).

Being, by projecting a "part" of Itself, manifests a "second" having the function of fertilizing matter or substance. *Vedānta* speaks of *puruṣa* (active, positive principle) and of *prakṛti* (receptive or negative principle). In Alchemy we have Sulphur and Mercury, and Chokmah and Binah in the sephirotic Tree.

The positive pole constitutes the *essence* and gives impulse, stimulus and a start; the negative pole represents the *substance* which, in turn, manifests indefinite universal forms through "sound", that is, vibration. Everything within the universe, including the human form, vibrates and the vibrating condition of a particular moment determines the state of its form. Over time, and according to some philosophies and theologies, this simple polarity became absolute duality to the point of being codified upon the moral plane as the forces of good and ill (moral or ethical dualism).

Existential planes also have this active-passive characteristic; the upper is active towards the plane below it. Within the *Vedānta* Vision there are three universal planes of existence: *Īśvara* (causal body), *Hiraṇyagarbha* (subtle plane) and *Virāṭ* (gross plane). *Īśvara* is active in relation to *Hiraṇyagarbha* and this one is active with regard to *Virāṭ* which is passive-receptive.

3. In order to avoid absolute dualism, it is important to comprehend that the polarity derives from the primordial One and therefore it must be considered *sacred*. The whole manifest polarity, including the male-female of the human state, is the expression of the Divine, which radiates its power in full stimulating activity. We need to recognize that polarity is the product of oneness which originates upon a superior plane of being. By studying actual human polarity we can discover things that are of extraordinary importance in order to achieve awareness of the human being as a bipolar unit (male-female).

4. This demonstrates how manifestation works through correlated, interdependent

factors. We can actually say that manifestation may emerge when the two factors are active, each exerting its own productive peculiarity. We have seen that when essence and substance interact there is manifestation at all levels and degrees.

5. If we move on to examine the human being, which is what interests us here, we see that the function in question is the male-female one. The human being, considered in his totality, is not merely a physical body, from which this polarity emerges, but also has an emotional body, a mental body and a noetic intellectual body. Both the theological and the philosophical Tradition of Initiation tell us that he also has a spiritual body.

Thus, the human being has within himself various polarities and must take them into account when trying to relate to other humans.

How, for example, can a man and a woman, as polarities, interrelate to create accord, a harmony capable of giving rise to uplifting music?

We need to explain in some detail the structural constitution of the being in its psycho-physical and spiritual components in order to come to a conclusion and answer this question.

"If in the fire of love I flame thus hot
Upon thee, past all wont of mortal mood,
Forcing thine eyes' surrender, marvel not;

This comes of perfect sight, with power endued
To apprehend, and foot by foot to move
Deeper into the apprehended good."

Paradiso, V, 1-6

PSYCHO-PHYSICAL AND SPIRITUAL CONSTITUTION OF THE ENTITY

«I do not have any cognition of so many and famous disciplines; and I wished I had this cognition! But, as you know well, I know nothing; the one exception, just a small science: the Science of Love»

Plato

Teages, 128 b

6. Let us study the distinctive constitution of the human male-female and give some guidelines indicating how to create an accord which will reflect the Original Accord.

7. The human being, as we have seen, is composed of the following body-vehicles:

a. The dense physical

b. The emotional sensorial

c. The mental analytical

d. The intellectual noetic

e. The spiritual

It is possible to be polarized especially within the physical-mental, or the emotional-physical, the intellectual or the strictly spiritual spheres. Thus, there are mental analytical beings almost devoid of emotions and feelings, or passionate sentimental beings whose discerning and analytical skills are limited. Furthermore there are the wilful, passive, introvert or extrovert types; then there are those who are particularly egocentric; there are the idealists and their opposites, the pragmatists, the materialists, and so on; it is always a question of polar aspects.

This first analysis is extremely useful in order to understand other beings, male or female; and could result in many misunderstandings being avoided from the beginning.

A couple must observe each other, comprehend each other's vehicular structure and the energy qualities they express.

8. The dense physical expresses the fundamental instincts of the species: sexual instinct, instinct for life at the formal or material level, the maternal or paternal instinct, the self-preservation instinct, and so on.

What is sex when considered as a phenomenon of organic reproduction?

It is constituted by anatomic and physiological characteristics which distinguish the individuals of the same species, therefore we speak of the male and female sex.

Thus defined, sexual differentiation is an attribute of numerous living organisms and is related to sexual or gametic reproduction, as opposed to a-gamic, or vegetative reproduction.

The male sex produces germinal cells (gametes) that are small and extremely mobile (micro-gametes or spermatozoa); the female produces larger-sized gametes (macro-gametes or ova). Sexual reproduction consists in uniting a male and a female gamete (fertilization). Whenever the two aspects of polarity meet there is creation.

This phenomenon of reproduction is exclusively inherent to the physical or corporeal element.

Seen however from a metaphysical point of view it is symbolic of that "embrace" between Heaven and Earth that gives birth to all beings. It is the representation of Harmony, of the conjunction of opposites, it is the portrayal of *puruṣa* and *prakṛti* reconstituting the primordial androgynous state.

9. On the other hand, the emotional, sensorial element expresses a complete range of emotions, feelings and desires; this element produces the attraction-repulsion polarity.

What is a feeling? It is a strong affection for a person, which is expressed by the urge to do him/her good. In this sense feeling, which responds to that conveyed by Plato's *filía* (φιλία), is a natural inclination caused by an attraction towards the pleasant (be it people, things or events).

Feeling is an appeal, a *desire* of the soul which binds two people; it is a fragrance which flows from an individual towards another or towards a particular thing, moved by a *desire* for enjoyment.

Again, it is the restlessness of the soul when facing an attractive person or object.

What must be underlined is that feeling, be it an inclination or desire towards a given object, involves contact, relationship and need; but every relationship implies *duality* and this, due to its dynamics, sooner or later creates pain.

10. The mental analytical body manifests intellectual discrimination and rationality, conditioned, however, by the empirical ego; therefore, we may be unilateral, lacking in objectivity, markedly cerebral and intellectual; its polarity is subject-object.

Idealism, which at times results in fanaticism, is an amalgamation of emotion-feeling and concept-idea.

11. Intuition has two possible pathways to pursue: the sensorial one concerning the particular or the supra-conscious that expresses universal ideas: this is pure intellect. The former refers above all to science or to questions of form, objects or matter; the latter is relevant to universal principles and to philosophical and metaphysical problems that are beyond the contingent or relative dimension. This is the Intellect of Love of which we shall speak later.

12. The spiritual concerns the strictly noumenic state which transcends both the particular and the universal because it is the sphere of Being in that it is and does not become. The polarity is between the entity and the Divine.

The approach to the spiritual may take two forms: the emotional-passionate from which religious *feeling* as such stems, and the more intellectual-intuitive supra-conscious one which is motivated by the need for realization and where spiritual Knowledge prevails.

These are the two pathways: the mystical one (in the western sense of the word) and the initiatory one. In the East these two ways are called *bhakti* and *jñāna* or gnôsis, or *aparavidyā* and *paravidyā* (non-supreme and supreme knowledge).

13. These, in synthesis, are the qualities expressed by the various body-vehicles or aspects of the human being. From this it may be deduced that a vehicle manifests *qualities*; therefore, a being is quantity

(body cell), but it is also and above all an expression of qualities.

Generally speaking man is conceived as the personification of body and mind, or body and psyche. Actually, to the materialist, he is only a body, and all qualities are mere "secretions" of hormones, cerebral cells, etc. But the body is *necessity*; thus the individual is forced to accept a life of *need*, hardship and poverty, not of pure Love.

Fortunately, however, man is not only this incomplete part, he is much more. For this reason we must examine the question from another point of view and complete the picture so that we may begin to outline the Science of Love.

"But awe, which still can daunt me with a mere
Ice or Be, again bowed down my head
As man's head droops down when sleep is near.

Not long Beatrice left me thus, but said,
With such a smile as would bring happiness
To one laid on the martyr's burning bed.

Paradiso, VII, 13-18

THE UNITY-TRINITY OF THE BEING

«Spirit, Soul and Body are but a unity of consciousness operating upon multiple states of Being. But we must also say that the generated is less than the generator, or the effect is less than the cause; the Spirit contains in itself the Soul and the Body, and in its undivided unity it is a perfect whole in itself beyond time-space and cause».

The Threefold Pathway of Fire, I, I, 96

14.   According to what is called "Philosophia Perennis", the human condition involves the following structure:

Body – Soul – Spirit

The Body is the gross-physical, the Soul is characterized by the noetic, intuitive mind and the Spirit is a spark of the Divine itself or Being. In ancient Greece the human being was seen as composed of *sôma*, *psyché* and *pnêuma*.

The hermetic Tradition speaks of Salt (physical Body), Mercury (Soul) and Sulphur (Spirit). In order to realize pure consciousness, it proposes three stages which correspond to the alchemical *opus*: the separation of the Mercury from the Salt, the fixation of the Mercury and finally the solution of the Mercury in the Sulphur. In this final phase Love is a law unto itself[1].

Religious, spiritual and initiatory traditions the world over all portray the question of the being's constitution in similar terms. Let us now seek to go more deeply into the problem in order to get a better grasp of distinct expressions of energy and understand where the human entity's forming is lacking.

Let us take another look at the conception of the human being previously described, which, with some additional details, may be summed up in the following table:

	Bodies	*Spheres*
Individuality World of the ego	Physical Emotional Mental	Particular Individual
Personality World of the Self or of the Ontological I	Intelectual Noetic or Intellect of Spiritual Love	Universal

36

Traditional Philosophy suggests that the human entity, through an act of free will, has cut itself away from the universal and, no longer being a *whole*, has reduced itself to a state of limited ego-individuality. This separation (some religions speak of a "fall") caused man to become twofold, therefore finding himself in an alienated position.

The individualized part of the ego being *incomplete*, "poor" by nature and weighed down by needs which it cannot satisfy on its own and opposed to the other ego, seeks the source of its satisfaction or completion elsewhere. In other words, it begins searching along the horizontal line and outside of itself for what it should look for and find within itself, conquering back that universal dimension from which in theory it broke away, and in which it would find the source of salvation and the re-establishment of the *Whole*.

As long as an entity, as simple individuality, is so "halved", and because the other individuality, towards which his gaze is directed, is also upon the same plane and in the same plight as itself, it can never fill the gap, however much it may desire it; two voids, two imperfections can never make a whole.

That is why, as long as one is individuality, or a psychological empirical ego, one is a prey to the desire for compensation, for possession of others and for acquisition of all kinds of objects, in order to make up for the impoverished state in which the ego has placed itself.

Therefore, as long as man moves within the bounds of individuality or of an ego qualified by instinct, emotions, feelings and passions and by separating-distinguishing thought, he can neither express nor understand Love, which by its nature is the exact opposite of the acquisitive ego.

Look up with me, then, Reader, to the reel
The exalted heavens tread, and scan that part
Where one wheel crosses with the other wheel;

There gaze enamoured on Master's art,
Whence never He removes the eye of Him,
Such is the love He bears it in His heart.

Paradiso, X, 7-12

THE CONCEPTION OF LOVE

«Socrates unveiled this *sacred mystery of Love* to Plato; and Plato, philosopher pious above all others, composed a book on it for the benefit of the Greeks»

Marsilio Ficino

From a writing addressed to
B. del Nero and A. Manetti

15. We are accustomed to speak quite naturally about sexual, emotional, filial love, love for life, for animals or for games, etc. But using the word "love" in reference to these qualitative aspects does not seem appropriate, or else we have identified love with our lower instincts, with desire, lust and coveting. In such a situation, we would have Love, with a capital letter, mixed up with desire which is a simple and even unstable psychological state. Thus, it is necessary to distinguish between the desire of an individual without possessions (and this gives rise to the craving to own and to possess) and Love that because it has, it can give; because it owns, it can offer; being full and complete, it can express itself and donate.

For example, when we say that we love someone, we mean that we desire her/him, and if the object of our desire disappears or opposes our desire, this gives rise to conflict and frustration.

We have seen that sexuality as an end in itself is not love, but a simple instinct of the species which at times takes the form of craving and a yearning to possess the object of our sexual appetite in order to relieve our energetic tension; from this point of view a partner becomes an *instrument* we use to satisfy our needs.

> «... it is not easy for the corrupt man to go from here to there, towards pure objective Beauty, when he contemplates beautiful things which receive the name from it. He looks, and his soul is not flooded with a generous impetus of veneration. It is all a matter of lust; like a four-footed beast he mounts and begets children. He has no scruple whatsoever and is not ashamed to have recourse to violent means...»[2]

Love may be expressed also at the sexual level, but this is not an essential aspect, because it can exist without the sexual act as such.

Some theologians consider "sensual love" mere instinct, even denying it the name Love.

16. The unbridled mind focuses its attention upon sex to such an extent that it completely influences the related energies and organs, while it considers the sexual act as inseparable from Love; and thus, it believes that sex is Love and Love is sex.

This has caused, and causes, a belittling of the nature of Love which, on the contrary, has an infinite range of expressive possibilities and may take any number of highly creative directions. Before being either male or female, we are entities, Souls, powerful focal Points of Being who, in time and space, and in a particular physical incarnation, can choose whether to be biologically male or female. Unfortunately attention is placed exclusively upon the male or female factor rather than on the soul as focal Point, which is the only aspect capable of comprehending the reasons behind the choice and of giving meaning and a basis to sexuality as a polar fact and as a highly specialized qualitative element.

17. If beings were programmed exclusively according to their sex it would be impossible for them to perform any act that was not already included in the nature of sexuality. Besides, an excessive population increase would represent a disaster for the planet, because of its space limitations.

On the other hand, both males and females are conditioned by a culture which makes the individual's identity dependent on sexual performance; so when this begins to fail, both man and woman feel that their identity is fading, which can cause serious damage at the psychological level. This may result in behavioral degeneration, which at times assumes truly pathological forms. As we have seen, before being males or females we are men and women and, above all we are Souls, whose nature is far removed from the merely sexual factor.

What today we call primitive society was based on far fewer preconceptions and was much less conditioned by the powerful positivist thought-form which "progressive" civilization has produced and developed. So-called primitive people could live in a completely free community because sex was relegated only to specific functions; they were not unilaterally obsessed by it. At that time the birth of a child was not, in an exclusive and reductive way, considered the progeny of a specific mother and father, but as the offspring of nature with which there was perfect symbiosis. They felt nature as an extension of themselves and therefore they considered themselves as elements interacting with it. Thus there was no separation between the ego and the environment, but consciousness knew how to embrace the surrounding world in an act of heartfelt identification. The energy of Love, even if not perceived objectively or considered as such, unified the different components of the existent whole.

18. Love is, therefore, a powerful unifying impulse, which transmits the grace of joy. Love floods and involves all it comes into contact with.

As the initiated Poet states, Love is a *propelling power* that "moves the sun and the other stars".

The miracle of Love allows growth, redemption and the expansion of consciousness to universal dimensions.

Love *sublimates* the sexual act because the intent comes from above and not from below, where it is prompted by instinct and need.

This implies that the act, made sacred, is adorned with sweet desire, by ecstatic contemplation and joyful and luminous glances which take root in Madonna Beauty herself, so that it creates beings that originate from the intelligible Heavens.

Love does not see the other as an object to possess or an instrument of mere enjoyment but as a subject to whom it offers itself; two polar hearts that love each other vibrate a joy and harmony which imparts rhythm to the space around them.

If all the couples on Earth loved each other with sublime Mind, the planet would emanate a different beam of *light* and have a different rhythm: it would become a *sacred planet.*

19. "Do you fear? Let us hold each other tight and we will be strong, stronger than the world and than the Gods. You know, one day a race of men inhabited the earth who were simply men that ignored the sweet union of Love.

And yet they were strong, so strong that one day they decided to attack the Heavens. Jove feared them and therefore he divided them so that each of them became two new beings: a man and a woman.

It happens at times that two of them, who were once one, thanks to the power of Love, reunite, and thus become strong, stronger than Jove, stronger even than the primitive beings they once were, because the union of Love is the supreme strength» (Sören Kierkegaard).

«Are you, by any chance, a Lover who goes looking for his *immortal* Beloved? Do you want to be one and the same thing with the heart's Beloved who does not know time and dispels the mist of space? I will give you the sequence of the opus that will raise you to the Peak of Love-Beauty in itself»³

According to the Myth, in ancient times beings were but of one sex, children of the Sun. But as they were extraordinarily strong and sought to climb to the heights of Heaven, God himself, upset by this boldness, divided them into male *and* female; now, the means to reunite them is Love, so that they may become *whole* again.

It is worth recalling that Love, on the manifest plane, is that *Teaching* which resolves all the duality, contradictions and sufferings of the world. Jesus gave us "the key to the gates of the Heavenly Kingdom", and this key, according to Jesus himself, is Love.

Knowledge illuminates, clarifies and reveals, but it is born under the impulse of Eros-Love.

Cognitive illumination, or "Holy Wisdom", knows that all is One and that multiplicity is mere appearance, but the activation of such a truth is the work of

Eros-Love which unifies the subject and the object of knowledge.

«So then, from such a remote source stems the mutual love innate to man. Love leads back to the primeval condition; it seeks to make one of what is two, it seeks to cure human nature. As a result, each of us is but one part, one half of the whole man: a man split open like a sole. He once was one and now they are two. And so each of us is always looking for his other half»[4]

This passage and many more show how Plato's philosophy is an operative "mysticism", leading to a reconstitution of the *Whole*.

Eros mends the separation by bringing the being back to *pax profunda*. It is a philosophy with a precise purpose because it belongs to that true *Philosophia* which descends from Above. It is proposed to human beings, who have fallen into the plane of generation, for their salvation. All Plato's teaching is directed to the "fallen" individual in order that he may return to the source and the splendor of the Sun-Good.

In *Politéia* too we find the same purpose:

«Indeed; but, as it is natural, it is not like *turning* an oyster-shell on the good side, like children do. *It involves a conversion of the Soul* (ψυχή περιαγογή) *from a day resembling night to true day; a pathway leading on high, the pathway of Being: that medium which we can say is true philosophy»*[5]

All initiatory Traditions speak of a "revolution", a "conversion" of the Soul in order to achieve Unity.

The *Bhagavadgītā* states: «What is dark night for all beings, is waking for he who is master of himself; when it is waking time for all beings, it is dark night for the sage whose inner eye is opened»[6].

The Christian *Gospel* states: «Near God the wise is insane and the insane is wise».

20. Love is *comprehension*, which means embracing, involving, enclosing, understanding with intelligence, integrating the other, or any thing, and *integrating* it until *unity* is achieved. In comprehension all

the contradictions of the restless psyche are resolved, thus pacifying the Heart.

Comprehension is *divine Wisdom*. Comprehension cancels distances because it puts up no opposition. It does not criticize because it comprehends; it does not judge because it knows that everything is in its proper place.

Comprehension, rather than studying the mind of others, directly touches their consciousness, which cannot but open up and yield. Comprehension is not mental discursiveness because it descends from that realm where Intelligence shines, therefore it is a *state of consciousness* which responds appropriately and wisely to the stimuli which may be both external and internal to the individual.

Comprehension is Love in action; it is the sweet expression of the Heart.

21. Because it is rich, Love is *giving*; because it *has,* it can offer itself at all existential levels, freely, for the sake of donation.

On the contrary, acquisitive desire is the nature of the psychological ego, and, being lacking and poor, it desperately seeks to possess in order to compensate for the failings innate in its own structure.

Generally two entities do not love but desire each other because they feel the need to compensate for and fill each other's shortcomings; but, if they have nothing, what can they give?

And yet the germ of Love exists in them; there is within them the pure and gentle Madonna who shines with "virtue and knowledge". It is a question of evoking the Power within them which awaits activation, because in every human heart lies this divine Spark which, once reawakened and developed, bursts into irresistible flames capable of devouring the debris of incompleteness.

Love integrates the needy ego and transfigures it, just as the river is integrated and transfigured by the majesty of the ocean.

22.   Love is *life-giving*, unifying and growth-bestowing. Desire, which is a surrogate, a negative reflection of Love, creates

duality or differentiation because it glori-
fies the ego.

Love belongs to the Soul, desire to individuality and to the empirical ego, which,
being separated from its divine counterpart,
is forced into deprivation and is obliged to
wander about in search of gratification.

23. Love is *joy-beatitude* which does
not stem from taking (otherwise it would
be mere gratification) but from the act itself of offering, of giving. Love rejoices in
Love; Love thrives on Love, therefore it is
removed from all duality or individualized
relationships.

Unlike desire, which is necessity, Love
lives in and by its own essence because it
is *beingness*, which is the prerogative of the
nature of the Soul.

24. Love is *fullness*. This can be expressed
only when the entity, having quenched the
yearning to possess in order to compensate
for the destitution in which it is struggling,
"recomposes" itself and returns to its original
Wholeness. Fullness is the integral state of

the Soul as Person. Hence the beatitude that comes from being an accomplished being.

Only those who have reached peace of mind and brought into unity the manifold and discordant voices of imperfect and demanding desire, can be in a state of fulfilment and therefore in a condition to offer, concede and give.

According to St. Bernard and to Richard from S. Vittore, Love suffices unto itself, without desire for possession.

> «Can Love be in want of Love being itself Love?... Sensory love is nostalgia for the lost Paradise»[7]

25. Love is *freedom* because it does not bind, since it does not consider the other separate from itself. Desire demands, dictates conditions and takes possession in order to compensate, as we have seen, for what it lacks. Desire generates agitation, restlessness and anxiety because it expresses itself in a dimension that *is not*; and it will, therefore, never be able to express things that do not belong to its nature, no matter how intensely it may wish to do so.

Freedom offers certainty. All forms of jealousy and desire for possession stem from the fear of losing the object of desire; therefore behind desire lurks the nightmare of suffering. Love is freedom because, not being the child of necessity, it imposes nothing.

26. Love is a gentle *sound* which attracts and pacifies. Being an "influence" – a "current", according to Plato (*Cratilus*, 420 a-b) – it is also a vibration, a rhythm, a breath which penetrates, envelopes, contains, fulfilling the spirit which receives it. From this point of view, Love is the revelation of Harmony which is the right Accord with the polarity of life, and Accord is but the revelation of *tonal consonance*.

Just as in music, rhythm gives life to sound, so Love gives life to polar relationships; it produces the exact equilibrium of tension and relaxation which must follow one another in the right proportions. Just as harmony creates the musical intervals between two or more notes vibrating chords, similarly Love creates assonance and proper and balanced encounter between two noble hearts vibrating consonant and pleasant melodies which, in their turn, produce stability. This is the exact opposite of desire, which is unstable and fleeting.

Sensual love (desire) is devoid of rhythm and harmony because lust, the child of dissonance, lacks equilibrium, cadence and amiable timbre, and therefore cannot produce clear chords, nor can it render a relationship shining and bright.

A couple who express the kind of Love-Accord we have spoken of so far, represent a sound comparable to what Pythagoras defines as the Music of the spheres. The two polar notes involved enter into a harmonic relationship capable of touching life at other levels; so they are not closed and individualized tonal systems running along parallel lines and trying only to coexist, as normally happens. Each of the two possesses his or her own pitch, tone and color which, taken together, produce that kind of harmony and resonance, which is more than their mere arithmetical addition and becomes a new and higher vibration operating at extremely profound and creative levels.

This is an entity who achieves realization through a specific relationship of tones and who is aware of the unity of the underlying sound, that is, of the Love-Archetype. At this point it is the "inner ear" that perceives the tone, the power of Love and osmosis, both immediate and innocent.

The tones at this level are expressions of life in the various soul-notes and contain within them both number and value. Number is characterized by quantity, by the expressive power of Love or by the frequency of the vibratory state, capable of reaching considerable heights (thus we have beings who incarnate powerful universal Principles). Value represents the quality of Love or of the Principle itself.

At such heights of life expression, it is not the separating instinct of self-preservation that binds and joins, nor is it emotion-sentiment-passion, because the "separation" has been resolved; it is not the utilitarian mind, since the pure Intellect of Love operates according to universal values and not thanks to the grasping ego. Such a state of Love abolishes space and time so that we may speak of immortal Love. It is profound "aesthetics" which transfigures all acts, all words, all movement, and requires conceptual or mental *silence,* because the word is replaced by the *vibration,* which penetrates, surrounds and progressively unfolds Harmony, Accord and the Intellect of Love.

If we speak here of "tones" it is because, in actual fact, Love, by vibrating a specific *influence*, possesses an indefinite range of possible sounds and, therefore, of harmonics. The look of two vibrating Strings that have come together again reveals many nuances of tone which careful "hearing" perceives as the resounding power of ecstasy, which inebriates to the point of transcending the objectively contingent, so that the "world" disappears to our perception. The miracle of Love!

«... It is necessary for the seer to become first similar and like what must be seen, and then concentrate on the Vision. Just as the eye would not be able to look upon the sun without becoming solar, and thus the soul cannot contemplate Beauty without first becoming itself Beautiful»[8]

She was unsmiling, but, "Were I to smile",
Her words began, "thou wouldst become the same
As Semelè, burned to an ashy pile.

For, as thou knowest, with a brighter flame
As we ascend the eternal mansion's stair
My beauty's splendor glows...

Paradiso, XXI, 4-9

COUPLES AT DIFFERENT LEVELS
OF POLARITY

«Two souls, or two vibrating chords, that *come together* create such a Love-Accord, such a Harmony and Beauty as to exalt the expectant space»

The Threefold Pathway of Fire, I, II, 2

27. The polar union takes place upon the purely physical level when there is interrelationship at the instinctual level. This leads to mere coupling which lasts only for the few moments of intercourse and which may occur with any member of the opposite sex belonging to the same species.

The polar union occurs upon the emotional-sentimental plane when desire flares in both poles and a strong magnetic field is formed, which lasts as long as passion-desire continues: in the case of animals this state may last as long as the mating season and at the human level for as long as the force of attraction lasts, which may even be for many years.

Upon the mental plane, union depends upon common ideals, cultural interests, an intellectual pursuit, an artistic passion and so on. If the polar individualities involved are particularly advanced, such a union may last a very long time, even for an entire life-time, leading to a mutual and beneficial maturity. In this case agreement is more harmonic because dialogue plays the main role. It is obvious that there can be unions of a mixed energetic nature, but in any case either the emotional-sentimental or mental focus prevails.

Upon the plane of the Intellect of Love the "active Intelligence" is at work and this gives off light and leads to contemplation, so that by means of union one may "see" the pure Idea of Beauty revealed in the human form. Here the question is not of culture, of erudition, of simple expression of concepts in which we still find personal feelings or individual points of view. Hence, we may deduce that there is a union of Souls, rather than of bodies or individualities, which can last even beyond the "death" of the physical vehicle.

Two Souls reunited in such a way give off "light" and "heat" on all planes and, although still two, they are in reality a sole self-sufficient being.

We can by right speak of Souls upon the same qualitative "beam" and in such cases biological age is of little importance. It is therefore possible to understand how the ideal union embraces all of a being's body-vehicles, because the upper integrates the lower. It may be said that in such a state the two beings emerge from the collective unconscious of the "human species" and travel on the wings of Love-Wisdom which knows no separation, no doubt and no uncertainty.

Two beings that vibrate together in such a fashion can "put to music" intelligible tonal principles and open the ears of receptive human beings; they can interpret the stupendous notes transmitted by the Great Universal Musician.

Because the *influence* is a vibration, Love vibrates rhythmic patterns, a sound which needs no words, as every state of consciousness is a "silent sound".

It may be noted that union upon the lower planes occurs between opposite sexes while, moving upward, union, although polar, occurs between kindred or similar beings who have like-minded dispositions and common aims which may be strictly intellectual or spiritual-metaphysical.

Let us remember, furthermore, that polarity is not absolute duality but complementarity.

28. We are speaking of a kind of *union* which should not be mistaken for simple animal copulation, nor with matrimony as such. Marriage is a legal contract and its operative dynamics are governed by the law for the sake of the family institution. Anyhow, it is obvious that union may lead to marriage, as may happen. However, it is important to distinguish between the two things because, as with organic intercourse, the difference is significant.

After them, my sweet Lady, as they flew,
Impelled me by one sign along the stair
My nature vanquished by her power anew.

Onearth,whereNaturespeedsmeneverywhere,
Aloft and down, no race or swiftest heat
Comparison with my ascent could bear.

Paradiso, **XXII**, 100-104

POLARITY WITHIN
THE HUMAN ORGANISM

«The individual is a combination of
seven main centers of Fire which, if
comprehended, coordinated, and integrated, can resolve into the sole Fire.
The mastery of this Fire implies having one's destiny in one's own hands»

The Threefold Pathway of Fire, I, I, 67

29. In addition to the polarity existing between persons of the opposite sex, there is also a polarity within the single individual. We have seen that the individual is composed of different bodies which express various qualities. The lower body is negative compared to the upper body; similarly, the dense physical body is negative compared to the emotional or sensorial one, while this, in turn, is negative when related to the mental body and so on. This helps us to comprehend why, when the emotional-sensorial body is stimulated, the physical one automatically responds. Similarly, when the upper intellectual body is stimulated, the lower vehicles, which are negative or receptive towards it, respond.

These events, occurring within the single individual, are important because in order to perform any activity whatsoever or to express an emotion, a concept, etc., a polarity is needed. Polarity is the source of becoming in all its manifold manifestations.

The constitution of matter owes its origin to a polarity composed of electrons (negative pole) and protons (positive pole). Manifestation is the effect of polar interrelationship, but life is, nonetheless, one.

30. At this point we can draw a summary of the various polarities existing within the individual's different bodies:

Body	Polarity	Creative aspect	Medium of connection
Physical	Male Female	Organic creativity	Reproductive organs Sacral center
Emotional	Attraction Repulsion	Relational creativity Rapport	Solar plexus
Mental	Subject Object	Intellectual creativity	Center of the throat
Noetic or of Love	Individual Universal	Pure reason All-including Love	Center of the brow

With reference to the media of connection we have expressed ourselves in terms of plexuses, which leads us back to traditional *Yoga* teaching. According to this Teaching, we are endowed with seven principal centers (*cakra*) situated along the back-bone. These centers are wheel-like and have the task of attracting energy and then channelling it to the organs. This energy is super-physical or pranic (*prāṇa*) and the centers are situated not in the physical but in the subtle or vital body, which is the more elemental form of dense matter. It is pure energy compared to the dense physical body, which is the mass.

Here is a list of the seven *cakra*-centers and their polarities at the physical level:

Center-cakra	Gland
Head (*Sahasrāra*)	Pitituary
Brow (*Ājñā*)	Pineal
Throat (*Viśuddha*)	Thyroid
Heart (*Anāhata*)	Thymus
Solar Plexus (*Maṇipura*)	Liver-pancreas
Sacral (*Svādhiṣṭhāṇa*)	Gonads
Coccyx (*Mūlādhāra*)	Adrenal glands

Polarity

75

As one who squinnies and by hook or crook
Will strain his eyes to see the sun's eclipse,
And, looking long, can then no longer look,

So I became, probing those fiery deeps,
The while I heard: "Why treatest thou so ill
Thy sight, seeking in me what thy world keeps?

Paradiso, XXV, 119-123

THE CONFIGURATION OF THE ENTITY
ACCORDING TO THE CAKRA

«The individuated material Fire works
through the *maṇipura cakra* (sensorial
solar plexus), the *svādhiṣṭhāṇa* (sacral
center-sexual energy) and the *viśuddha*
(mental center) which acts under the influence of the first two centers. The radiant
Fire works through the center of the heart
(*anāhata*) and *viśuddha* center which,
in this case, is under the influence of the
anāhata cakra. The spirit of incorruptible
Fire acts through the center *ājñā*: the Eye
of Śiva»

The Threefold Pathway of Fire, I, I, 70

31. The *mūlādhāra cakra* expresses combative energy and stimulates the adrenal glands which, in turn, charge the bloodstream with adrenaline. This is mainly energy of the physical order and its task is to safeguard the body-form. *Kuṇḍalinī* (pranic energy) is located in this *cakra* and, when aroused, liberates the alert disciple, while it enslaves the unwary neophyte who is not sufficiently purified.

In the case of an advanced being, this *cakra* is negative vis à vis the *ājñā cakra*. Unfortunately, in the case of the majority of people who do not follow the Science of Love, this *cakra* assumes a positive value.

The *svādhiṣṭhāṇa cakra* expresses the energy which urges sexual union, cause of the reproduction of the species, and in psychological terms it reveals restlessness, the need to acquire things of all kinds; it is associated with the *mūlādhāra cakra*. It is negative with regard to *viśuddha* in the case of the advanced disciple but positive in the case of the unpurified novice.

If associated with the *viśuddha cakra,* it may supply vital and even creative impulse to the empirical mind; if, on the contrary, it is separated from its corresponding upper *cakra* and from the heart center (*anāhata*), sexual energy acquires such furious strength that it can express itself as violence, especially in the male, leading to irresponsible acts as well as to significant sexual deviations.

The *maṇipura cakra* expresses the energy of affection, of desire, of feelings; in fact its *bīja* or seed is *Ram*, in this case the symbol of individualized or egoic fire. This *cakra* is negative vis à vis the heart center in the advanced disciple but positive in the case of the unpurified aspirant.

As we can see, the aim of the disciple is to render the three lower *cakra* (plexus, sacral and coccyx) negative, the upper ones (heart, throat and brow) positive. At the beginning of the pathway the petals of the *cakra* of the heart are turned downward to feed the three lower *cakra*; in the advanced disciple these petals are turned upward to feed the upper *cakra*. All things considered, the purpose of the disciple on the path is that of reversing the polarity of the *cakra*.

The Soul, which at the moment of the "division" turned its attention towards the three lower *cakra* (the petals of the heart are turned downwards), later "takes flight" and directs its attention towards the three upper *cakra* (upturning of the heart petals).

In the case of the advanced disciple, the *ājñā*, which is related to the upper mind, synthesizes the various *cakra* under the aegis of the heart center (the seat of the incarnate Soul, whose vehicle of manifestation is pure intellect). When it is guided by the solar plexus or *maṇipura*, the center of the throat (*viśuddha*), being the seat of the sense of ego, expresses mental energy or empirical-formal and therefore acquisitive thought. If on the other hand it is directed by the center of the heart (and therefore becomes positive with regard to the *svādhiṣṭhāṇa cakra*), it is absorbed by the pure Intellect of Love (*ājñā*) and, therefore, becomes universal mind, because it includes the Whole. It is only at this stage that one can undertake the pathway of all-including Love.

The awakening of the *sahasrāra* or thousand-petalled *cakra* leads to total liberation of all energy, synthesizing all polarities. As we have seen, the union of opposite principles, the "mystical Marriage" (Śiva-Śakti) is accomplished within the same being. And because it concerns male and female polarities or elements, this union is considered as "incest" in the alchemical doctrine (and not only there).

Therefore, all beings are divided into male and female as such; then into male and female united by polarity under the impression of Love. Finally they are the male and female element within the same individual (divine hermaphrodite). This is the Great Teaching which is also the *Sacred Mystery* as expounded by Plato in the *Symposium* of Love.

«... from two, to become one. And the motive? Our ancient structure was this, we were *whole.* To the burning aspiration for the primeval totality and the effort to attain it anew is given the name of Love»[9]

There is a text by Averroës (Ibn Rushd) called *About the Beatitude of the Soul and its Marriage with Abstract Intelligence,* where the Author maintains that the greatest level of beatitude is achieved through the highest degree of ascent, which coincides with marriage through Love. When this union occurs, the highest degree of ascent is reached. This brings us back to Plato, to the *Canticle of Canticles,* to the "Fedeli d'Amore", where the Intellect of Love is portrayed in an ecstatically beloved "Woman" or a "Rose", and to the mystics of ancient Persia and so on.

As a final consideration within this brief overview on polarity, we can say that we share the three lower *cakra* with the so called animal kingdom, while we share the three upper *cakra* with the world of... the Gods, or with states that transcend our individualized states.

"Begin then: say to what thy soul clings fast,
Be reassured and rid thee of fear's bias;
Thy vision is not dead but overcast.

She who escorts thee through this bless'd and pious
Region, holds in her gaze such power to heal
As once was in the hand of Ananias".

Paradiso, XXVI, 7-12

EROS IN GREEK MYTHOLOGY

«I invoke the great, pure, lovable and sweet Eros, winged archer, flaming and forceful on attack, who plays with both the gods and mortal men, industrious, double-natured, who holds the keys to all... O blessed one, come down to the initiated with pure thoughts, and drive away base and vile desires from them»

Orphic Hymns, *To Eros*

32. An ancient Greek myth tells us that Eros appeared in order to render the earth fertile. Before, all was silence, emptiness and immobility. Now all is life, joy and animation.

According to Orphism, Eros is that original and powerful creative force which moves the entire cosmos. It is the divinity that drew the orderly cosmos from the primitive Cháos.

Cháos is uncontained Space which contains all that exists, therefore it is of the metaphysical order; it is the quabbalistic Great Ocean, it represents the primordial Waters that are activated when Eros awakens to create the upper Waters (the intelligible world or plane) and the lower Waters (sensorial plane). Cháos is also the cause underlying the five subtle and gross principles.

Thales himself drew on this myth, or traditional Knowledge, when he defined Water as the Mother of all created things.

For ancient Greece, Ocean was the father of the Gods. Plato too speaks of intelligible *kóra* (χώρα) and sensible χώρα as the universal Mother-space from which all bodies, from the simple to the compound, from the smallest to the greatest, are formed. This is the equivalent of *prakṛti* in *Vedānta*.

In other contexts Cháos is compared to the Cosmic Egg (another symbol common to all traditional cosmogonies). This is the primordial Egg (for *Vedānta*, *Hiraṇyagarbha* or Golden Egg) generated by Night, whose two halves form the Earth and the Heavens, that is, the sensible and the intelligible planes.

In the Egyptian *Book of the Dead* (chapter LIV) we read: «O Tum! Let me breathe the vivifying air welcome to your nostrils! Because I am the Egg of the cosmic Ocean».

The first element born of the primordial Egg is life-giving Air (Anaximenes considers Air the origin of life). In *Vedānta* this is *ākāśa* which is also assimilated into living Fire. Anaximander goes even further because, when interpreting the concept of Cháos, he states that *Apeiron* is the non-qualified principle (*arché*) not determined as far as quantity and non-qualified; that is to say, the Infinite. Thus, with the passage from Myth to Logos, Ocean, Cháos, the Waters etc. become the Infinite from both the "spatial" and "qualitative" points of view. Thus conceived, the Infinite is the state which precedes manifestation[10].

Therefore, the God who first emerged from Night and gave *vitality* and movement to existence was Eros, often identified with non-substantial Fire, who, in turn, produced substantial Fire (*ākāśa*), but of the intelligible order. He is all vital Electricity, the Zoroastrians' sacred Fire, Hermes' Fire, Cibele's Shaft and Apollo's flaming Torch. In the *Zend Avesta* it is written: «A Fire which offers the possibility of knowing fire».

Thus Eros is an impulse overflowing with Love which leads existence from potentiality to act.

Identified even with Zeus, father of all the Gods, Eros breathed into the bodies of man and woman and infused into them the vital breath, therefore he is the bestower of life; this breath infuses Soul in the bodies so as to animate them;. In *Occidental Mythology,* Joseph Campbell observes that Eros is the progenitor, the original creator from which all life begins.

«Great God is Love. A marvellous God amid men and Gods, and for many reasons. Birth above all. He, mark you – continued Phaedrus – can boast of being the eldest of the Gods. Here is the proof. Love has no parents; no prose-writer or poet has ever affirmed that he had any. But Hesiod says that first there was Cháos: "but then broad-bosomed Earth, a safe haven for all, and Love". And Acusilaus agrees with Hesiod and states that after Cháos came Gea and Eros... And Parmenides speaks of the generation of the Gods: "First in the train of Gods, he moulded Love"»[11]

For Marsilio Ficino Eros «... gives life to dead things, forms the informal, gives perfection to what is not perfect»[12].

33. Throughout the ages Eros, although with features quite unlike those of the original Myth, has been considered as an expression of the primordial Energy of the universe, which not only guarantees the continuity of the species, but represents the basis of cosmic *cohesion*.

As the initiator of life, not only at the formal level, Eros-Love operates through:

– the law of directional *Dynamic Will*, in order to give proper and intelligent direction to the development of life; it is "tension" towards unity of Purpose;

– the law of *Attraction,* in order to create reciprocal magnetic interrelations between all cosmic elements, be they beings or forms (each vital element is attracted by the other and together they are attracted by the Principle).

Will, Attraction or attractive action and Knowledge-illumination correspond to the three aspects of the *Śiva-Śakti* of the

Vedānta Tradition: *icchā* (will); *kriyā* (action); *jñāna* (knowledge).

– The law of *Cohesion* in order to unite and strengthen the totality of life. Thus Eros prompts macro and microcosmic polar union in order to perpetuate manifestation. As the power of Attraction and of Cohesion, Eros links all living things, tends to overcome all antagonism and to assimilate apparently diverse forces and tendencies by integrating them into the same unit.

Therefore, Eros is the symbol of *coincidentia oppositorum* as he reconciles opposites, even bitter enemies; Shakespeare had this in mind when he used the love between Romeo and Juliet to overcome the rivalry between the Montague and Capulet families and thus bring unity and peace to the city of Verona.

Eros-Love operates also through:

– The law of *Luminous Radiation*, which originally represented the *Fiat Lux* which gave "light" and "heat" (therefore: light, sound, life) to all things. From this point of view Eros is Fire, in all its various modes; even the human being's cognitive illumination or divine Wisdom is an aspect of Eros' Fire.

Furthermore, during the last cycle of manifestation, Eros-Love expresses himself through the law of *Unification*, bringing the many back to the One.

34. It is always Eros who initially causes the disciple to "lose" himself within the meanders of differentiation (the *desire* to be the many). Later, Eros, availing himself of the laws of Cohesion, Illumination and Unification, leads the disciple back from the multiple to the ontological One, and then to the metaphysical One.

35. Even Freud views Eros as opposed to the instinct of destruction and considers the purpose of Eros as that of preservation and of a growing tendency towards cohesion and unity. This brings to mind Empedocles' two principles: Love and Contention, seen, naturally from a cosmic point of view.

According to Rollo May (*Love and Will*), «Eros is the fulcrum of a culture's vitality, its heart, its soul. When creative Eros vanishes and vital tension fails, then a civilization begins to decline»[13].

Love-Eros is both an ontological spring and a source of realization; it is the foundation that causes effective union between man and woman. As we have already seen, desire represents the urge to possess, and this is a cause of division rather than of union and cohesion. There is no greater betrayal than when a part or a pole claims the right to be all, the whole. One could unconsciously arrive at a loving solipsism.

36. The true erotica (ἐρωτική) for Plato is the Art and Science of Love and represents that particular pathway which, availing itself of illumination and Beauty, leads to the Absolute and supreme Good. Thus Eros, at certain levels, "offers wings", that is, elevates and becomes the medium unifying the Soul with the Absolute.

Unfortunately later thought and especially modern thought brings the idea of Love and Eros down to the level of passion and sex, abandoning the concept of pure Love and of the God as giver of Life. This has led to a decline in Traditional Knowledge and to the prevalence of a merely animal conception of Eros.

"The Primal Light the whole irradiates,
And is received therein as many ways
As there are splendours wherewithal it mates.

Consider well the breath, behold the height
Of His eternal Goodness, seeing that o'er
So many mirrors It doth shed Its light,

Yet One abideth as It was before."

Paradiso **XXIX**, 136-138, 142-145

THE PLATONIC EROS

«Among the Gods Eros is the most
ancient, the most august, the most
apt to render men virtuous and
happy, both in life and in death»

Plato

Symposium, 180 b-c

37. With Plato, Eros as the God who set manifestation in motion and with his arrow (positive pole) caused the earth (negative pole) to generate, takes on an apparently different function. The philosopher transposes Eros as the means of elevation and solution of the state of misery in which the human being, fallen into generation, finds himself. Thus Eros, as the son of Póros and of Penia, is seen as having a double nature.

The word Póros (Πορός) is usually translated as "rich" or "ingenious", but in the traditional and even literary context it indicates: the means by which to cross the ford, the passage, even the pathway, the means by which to reach something. The verb περάω indicates going, carrying, bringing. The Father of Eros is, therefore, he who "ferries", who is capable of "carrying" people somewhere or he who offers a passage, a ford; in other words, he who acts as a "bridge".

Penia (Πενία), from the verb *penomai* (πένομαι) which means "to toil", "to work" or "to be in need" or "wanting", is the Mother and she corresponds to the *kóra* (χώρα) of which all body-forms are made. She is wanting because, having Póros as a basis, she is not whole. The sensible separated from its metaphysical essence (ουσία) cannot exist.

Plato's Eros has something of the sensible (which is incomplete due to its non-being) and of the intelligible because the Father, in order to be the "bridge", must find himself in such a state.

Besides, Eros reflects the condition of the Soul which lives two seemingly contradictory aspects: there is the Soul as such, which is of divine, noetic and paternal origin and therefore capable of expressing all intelligible potentialities and there is its "reflection", which has fallen on to the plane of generation through an act of free will (due to "temerity", according to Plotinus). This reflection lives in a state of misery, want and restlessness, having identified with the formal substance, with "matter", with χώρα or *prakṛti* (according to *Vedānta*); that is to say, with the "mother". Eros prompts the Soul (*psyché*) to reintegrate its "reflection", its fallen "part" and then take flight towards its noetic essence (*Noûs*).

Thus, for Plato, Eros is the helmsman who, availing of the "Science of Love", ferries the Soul across from formal or sensible love to intelligible love-Beauty.

Once the need for gain, which offends and mortifies, has been erased, the entity, immersed in unfathomable, all-exalting Beauty, may sail towards the splendor of the spiritual Sun (*Noûs*). We may say that Plato's Eros is only one aspect of the Eros-God of ancient Orphic Theogony; the aspect which urges us towards Wisdom, Beauty and noetic Love.

We have seen that Eros possesses the nature of Love but also that of Wisdom and the two are really one. Eros may therefore be interpreted as being that Holy Wisdom of which the "Fedeli d'Amore", that confraternity of initiated poets, spoke. Wisdom-Love is personified by a "woman": Beatrice for Dante, Giovanna or Monna Vanna for Guido Cavalcanti, Lagia for Lapo Gianni, Madonna Intelligenza (Lady Intelligence) for Dino Compagni, Selvaggia for Cino da Pistoia, and so on.

Dante's *Vita Nova* and his *Convivio* (an obvious reference to the work of the same name by Plato) concerns Dante's initiatory experience together with the "Fedeli d'Amore" group. Dante, Guido Cavalcanti and the others point out to us that Holy Wisdom springs from the Intellect of Love which, according to Guinizelli, resides in the *gentle* (medieval Italian: gentile = pure) heart:

«Love always returns to the gentle heart»[14]

The Intellect of Love is at work within the "Fedeli d'Amore" because they have received initiation. «Women who have Intellect of Love» concerns those belonging to the Order because the word "Woman", besides representing Love-Wisdom, was often used by extension to indicate a member of the Confraternity.

The concept of two-fold Love was also taken up by this initiatory Current. It mentions a first form of love directed towards the senses and a second Love towards *Contemplation*; the former is full of desire and passion and pulls the soul downwards, whereas the latter raises it up to the "Angelic Contemplation" of Love which is represented by the Woman.

Here is how Guido Cavalcanti expresses the idea:

«I see in the eyes of my Woman
a light full of spirits of Love
that carry a new pleasure to the heart
such that arouses new happiness of life»[15]

The "Fedeli d'Amore" quenched their thirst at the "Fontana dell'Insegnamento" [The Font of Teaching] mentioned by Dante; this Font is none other than the initiatory Tradition.

Plato too "sings" of his Woman: Diotima, who initiates him in the sublime Science of Love.

Diotima is the incarnation of Love-Wisdom and as such may initiate Plato into the Mysteries of Love, just as Beatrice, the incarnation of Love-Wisdom, initiates Dante, making him a "Fedele d'Amore".

We are not the only ones to hold that the Science of Love is one of the profound currents of initiation which, since the dawn of history, has offered and still offers men who have fallen into generation the possibility to redeem themselves.

It is an underground current which, in certain ages or in particular circumstances, comes back to light to be proposed once again. It is sufficient to recall that the *Canticle of Canticles*, attributed to Solomon and included in the Bible, is believed to be dated about the fourth century A.D. A similar vision of Love-Beauty-Wisdom inspired the Persian poets, (in addition to the symbol of "wine" and "beloved youth"; for this latter theme see Plato as well). Furthermore, through the Templars, this symbol entered the Langue d'Oc and Langue d'Oïl love poetry.

Jesus himself proposed the theme of Love as the foundation for one's own union with the Father, even if he presented it in exclusively mystical terms. However it is also held that the Science of Love of Jesus («I give you the *key* to open the Kingdom of Heaven») is summarized in specific and well-defined initiatory stages leading to identity with the Father: «I and the Father are one... Who sees me sees the Father». This obviously does not take into consideration all the theological-philosophical, dianoetic and sentimental interpretations proposed down through the ages.

In a traditional context *bhakti* (from *bhaj*) means active and loving *participation* in the transcendent or the Divine. Very often the term is translated as devotion where simple sentiment prevails; but in reality *bhakti* is much more, it is the expression of that Eros-Love which unites up to the realization of union with the Divine.

Therefore, by saying Love, Beauty, Wisdom or Eros we mean the very same thing. Just as Harmony is the result of the simultaneous intonation of two or more sounds which vibrate in consonant agreement and that appeal to the ear of the listener, so Beauty (τὸ καλόν) is the outcome of a blending of factors such as size, order, proportion, truth, etc. so that the eye and, therefore, the heart of the beholder, are enraptured.

> «So, the profound characteristic of Good has taken refuge within the constitutional *nature of Beauty*; in reality, measure and proportion resolve into Beauty and Virtue with no doubt at all... So, if we are unable to grasp *absolute Good* through a sole Idea, let us try to grasp it through three Ideas: *beauty, proportion, truth*»[16]

Eros-Love is powerful and impetuous, it is "all-inflaming Love" and urges the Soul, sundered from the intelligible, to return to its original state. Furthermore Eros and Psyché (Love and Soul) become two correlated terms: the Soul, as expression of Eros, generates forms (just as upon the macrocosmic plane it generates the whole formal manifestation) and Eros, as expression of the Soul, infuses thirst for transcendence.

38. Having contemplated Beauty in itself and Love in itself in the Hyperuranus sphere, or the World of pure Ideas, the Soul, by its own deliberate act of will, penetrates the corruptible bodies, *forgetting* its origin.

The remembrance of Love-Beauty comes about in a very special way, because alone amongst all other Ideas, only Beauty *is* «extraordinarily evident and extraordinarily lovable».

The splendor of Beauty in itself reflects in perceptible beauty lighting up and inflaming the Soul with so much purifying fire that it lifts it to the beatitude and delight of supreme Love and Beauty.

«... nothing is as capable as Love to infuse in us a similar yearning»[17]

39. Thus, for Plato, what is commonly indicated as sensible love is but a simple and modest flickering of Love because this

latter loves Beauty in its supra-egoic state. The true lover-philosopher is he who knows how to climb the various steps that lead up to the supremely beautiful Vision. On the other hand, once it has fallen into generation (even if only with one of its "beams" or "reflections"), the Soul finds it hard to fly all at once towards the world of pure intelligible Beauty and, complying with human nature, it must *open up* to contact with sensual forms. Love is love of beauty because above all it pleases *sight,* the most perfect of the senses.

The platonic Plotinus as well gives this indication:

«...let him depart from this point, from earthly love, and ask himself what pursuing that which is beloved more than anything else in the entire world can mean, and then consider that this is love of mortal, deadly creatures, love of phantoms, fleeting love, because its object is neither truly lovable nor is it for our good, nor is it what we really seek. Up there, on the contrary, is the true object of love, with which it is possible to be reunited, partaking in Him and possessing Him truly, and yet without exterior carnal embrace»[18]

Following this great platonic Master, we consider physical corporeal love which is expressed, through desire and lust, as an urge to possess a body, however lovely, as the lowest type of love. Higher up there is a stage where souls become inflamed with the divine spark of Love which leads to the dimension of the intelligible. Moving upwards, Love approaches the Beauty of the Gods, causing deification of Beauty and, still ascending through contemplation of the Idea of Beauty in itself as sole universal archetype, Love realizes the supreme Teaching, so that our Soul is united with the Idea. Then there is no more duality (which was only apparent) but the Idea of Beauty-Love prevails alone like a radiant Light that infuses Beauty into the lovers of Beauty.

How can the lover become like the Beloved, or beauty turn into Beauty? This is a question to which the divine Plato and with him all platonic lovers might answer by saying that the true entity, in its essence, and the Idea of being, are one and the same thing.

In this way writes Marsilio Ficino:

> «I ardently urge you to love this Light, as supreme Beauty... and Light in its essence is the infinite Beauty»[19]

In sensory bodies we love only the many "appearances", the copies of Beauty; in the Soul we love the radiant Light (Knowledge) which longs for the Beautiful because it contemplates Beauty; finally pure Being (*Noûs*), as Idea, transforms itself into Beauty in order to express the supreme Good. In this way, step by step, one passes from differentiation to oneness, from division to reunification with the Idea, from multiple beauty to Beauty-Good in itself. Thus, entities, lost within the dimension of generation and having become multiplicity, return to the undivided, whole state.

> «In fact, for people who want to live in a beautiful way, what must guide them for their entire lives is not kinship, honors, riches or anything else, as none of these can inspire in such a beautiful way as Love»

110

«... not all Eros is beautiful or worthy of being praised, but only that one that pushes us to love in a beautiful way»

«... is giving birth in beauty, both according to the body and to the soul»[20]

"But of these waters thou must drink", so spake
Mine eyes' own sun, whose light their solace is,
"Before so great a thirst as thine thou slake.

The stream", she added then, "the topazes
Which glitter in and out, the smiling shore
Are of their truth but shadows-prefaces."

Paradiso, **XXX**, 73-78

LOVE IS BEAUTY

«Love is Beauty bestowing happiness
devoid of possession and separation»

The Threefold Pathway of Fire, I, II, 5

40. We are aware of the fact that sensual love stems from what pleases, but pleasure is simply attraction towards beauty: it may be directed towards an object, a person or an event. Sensible beauty attracts, eliciting response. But the fact that we respond means that the idea of Beauty is already within us. All external stimulations can receive a response if the corresponding quality already exists within the human entity; thus the external factor is simply a symbol capable of *evoking* a response already in waiting.

As sensible pleasure is born of emotion-feeling, we can consider it of subjective origin; the same stimulus may evoke different responses and the same object may be beautiful to one person while it is not to another. Pleasure, according to Plato, is *becoming*:

> «In conclusion, as I was saying at the beginning of the reasoning, we should be grateful to he who revealed that pleasure is *generation* and *becoming*, and that it does not ever attain in the least nor for any reason the level of *being*»[21]

Even sexual energy itself, unless it is a simple release of tension, tends towards what is attractive, towards that beauty of form capable of stimulating a response. In such a dimension we find ourselves loving Beauty divided into the many forms of *becoming*, but one beauty amid many is not *the* Beautiful, before which *every* being falls into ecstatic contemplation.

If Love has the gift of perceiving Beauty, this is because Love itself is Beauty, otherwise it would not have the possibility of recognition. We can say that Love contains Beauty and that the latter contains the former.

> «Love is Beauty because Love is a dance which allows us to *savor* union, the *taste* of Being, intelligible Beatitude; it is supreme tonal accord of principles; Beauty is Love because Beauty is perfectly commensurable with the Idea, it is the fragrance of a joyful motion, the fulfilment of Universal Law and Order»[22]

116

41.   As already mentioned, if beautiful
things are so many and so varied there must
be a sole, ineffable Beauty hidden behind
them and of which they are but the "reflection". Thus, if there are many forms in
which beauty can be perceived, this implies
that there must be a common denominator,
in other words Beauty as prime factor or
archetype.

Therefore the numerous manifestations of
sensory beauty *participate* in the one and
only Beauty who towers above all the single forms of beauty and who dwells within
the supra-sensible dimension, where the archetype remains *constant*. Thus, beautiful
forms change and perish just like the love-
desires of human egos do, but true Beauty
does not, otherwise all sensible beauty would
also vanish with its source or principle.

Because of its affinity with the Idea, the
Soul vaguely feels within sensible form the
presence of something that goes beyond
form itself, and thus experiences a vibra-
tion-influence, an inspired fury (μανία)
which lifts and pulls it away from the world
of forms. This vibration also withdraws

the Soul from concrete analytical thought, which is unable to decipher the Idea of Beauty.

Beauty is the creation of Being conceived by the *norm* of the sublime, and so it is a vertical impulse.

> «Therefore, procuring *purifications and initiations to the mysteries*, this *manía* (influence)... made sane those who were sharing in it»[23]

And here is how the platonic Plotinus expresses himself:

> «There is, though, a transcendent beauty that *feeling* did not have the fate to attain, but the soul, even though without the sensory organs, sees and judges. And we have to, after having abandoned feeling waiting down there, ascend and contemplate»[24]

42. So that the Soul may grasp Beauty behind its formal reflection, one must be purified and must *contemplate*. In order to venture beyond sensible beauty, the Soul's most powerful tool is contemplation.

This implies development of the inner Eye which alone can recognize Reality behind appearance, can see intelligible Beatitude behind sensorial pleasure, which is but its shadow, and can recognize Beauty in itself behind a handsome body shaped by it. Contemplation alone is capable of penetrating the heavy mist of the sensible and, thanks to that particular and special Eye, of "seeing" the Principle, the Idea, the Maker, which renders all things beautiful.

A glance, a gesture, a movement, a word, the occurrence of an encounter, everything becomes gentle beauty if it is Beauty who looks, speaks and moves. To reach this condition, to go beyond transient beauty, it is not sufficient to acquire complex knowledge of an exclusively scientific kind, nor to delve into dianoetic speculation or even to follow moral rules. «Contemplate, though without throwing your thinking outwardly», says Plotinus.

The human entity must, therefore, purify himself and become initiated in Beauty in order to become "living contemplation".

«But if contemplation wanes, he can reawaken anew the virtue which dwells within him and by meditating on his being so perfectly adorned, he will find a gain his lightness and will ascend to the spirit through the way of virtue...»[25]

When one reaches this state, the contemplator becomes one with the object of contemplation, which is Beauty *per se*, thus transcending the beauty of non-being.

«If you see yourself thus, become, by now, "vision", if full of faith in yourself, although still down here, you reached the Sublime... oh! then, fix, still, your gaze. Because your eyes alone are contemplating grand Beauty»[26]

43. Disillusion and subsequent pain emerge because the human being has clung to the *desire* of form and to sensation, which appears and disappears, is born, changes and fluctuates because it is in the state of becoming.

Love, which is beauty of expression, harmony of color and perfection of Being, cannot bring disappointment or create conflict, as it is beyond duality. The desire for what is beautiful comes after response to the stimulus which beauty aroused. One desires because one has not, but Beauty, because it dwells in us, does not need to be sought or desired. The Beauty which is in us loves what is beautiful thanks to an act of *identity*. Unlike *desire*, this is a *direct* factor which is free from any kind of *discursiveness* or mediation.

«This fate was awarded to Beauty alone; in all clearly visible and worthy of immense love»[27]

«Beauty, as is presented through symbols (therefore with an enigmatic language) in the myth of the *Phaedrus*, is this bridge [that is Eros-Beauty]. A divine ray lost within the reign of becoming and pain. Beauty, the messenger of an absolute and perfect realm, through ascension may lead to the dizziest heights of the universal order. Beauty which feeling cannot grasp, not the other Ideas of justice and other virtues; Beauty bestowed upon the world with incredible plenty; Beauty which acts powerfully and irresistibly even upon the lower movements of the soul, those shared by all humans.

If Beauty were to act upon the higher movements only, its power of detachment would not be so complete. In actual fact, human beings, starting from the very first step of their spiritual experience, from the lowest step available to all, find themselves in the company of this mysterious Iris, harbinger of other heavens. And it is this same messenger who guides the selected few capable of ascending the stairway; it is always she who leads and accompanies, urges and elevates. Her face is gradually laid bare to reveal a more and more stunning mien, but it is always she, Beauty, the matron of honour at the secret nuptials of the supreme vision»[28]

Love and Beauty, as we have seen, do not represent duality but are oneness, they are the being's resolving, ultimate perfection.

Eros heats the icy *substance* of the intelligible entity's five-fold vehicle with the transfiguring power of Fire and the Soul lets itself float in the placid ocean of Love which nourishes lovers in an ecstasy of joy.

Eros is the God who ferries us over the sweet waters of Love to the very essence of Love, to the Idea.

Therefore it is not sufficient to extract from sensorial beauty the simple dialectical "concept" of the beautiful, one must know how to interiorize and experience that content within the intelligible dimension, where the essence of Beauty, or Beauty in itself, which coincides with the *summum bonum*, may be grasped.

«If some, therefore, fix their gaze upon Him who, although dispensing beauty to all remains Himself motionless, and although offering all receives nothing for Himself, if they remain *steadfast* in that contemplation, if they draw beatitude from that making themselves *similar* to Him, what beauty could one want? He, in fact, is supreme Beauty: He is that primordial Beauty which makes all His lovers beautiful and lovable»[29]

44. Plato leads us to the Initiation of Love (Love which all seek but often fail to find because they lack Wisdom, and therefore misdirect their energies) along a pathway which begins, as we have seen, with sensible love-beauty and ends with the realization of supra-sensible Love-Beauty, which

integrates and unifies the totality of Love-Beauty at all possible levels of expression.

A relationship between two incomplete egos leads sooner or later to conflict because there is no magnetic flow from the Intellect of Love. When this vehicle of the Soul, the ontological Ego or all-including Awareness is missing, we have a simple union of bodies, desire of one for another, interest and necessity and passion, but not that Love which leads to ecstasy.

Here is another table illustrating the various states of "profane" love (sensorial desire) and of intelligible inclusive love.

Empirical ego	{	Physical body Emotional body Mental body	Sensible Love
Ontological I Soul	{	Physical body Emotional body Mental body Intellect of Love	Intelligible Love

Thus, faced with sensible beauty in all its vital manifestations, the human being may take one of two directions: he may either stop to love the outward *resemblance*, the simple reflection of Beauty-Love, causing himself limitation and alienation and, sooner or later, inevitable tension or pain; or he may, by unveiling the Idea of Beauty which stands above all forms, ascend to intelligible ecstasy. The former kind of love is represented by popular or common Aphrodite, the latter by celestial Aphrodite. In this second state the Soul at last finds Beatitude, the supreme good.

«It does not seem to me, my friend Phaedrus, that the topic of this discourse has been properly formulated: just to praise Love thus, without reserve. If there were only one Love, then the formula would be appropriate. But there is not only one. And as there is not one alone, we must first decide which we must celebrate with our words.

I shall try to correct this error and determine, first of all, what kind of love we should praise; secondly, to celebrate these lauds in a manner befitting the God.

We all know that Aphrodite has always got Love as her companion. As a result, if the Goddess were one only then Love too would be one only. But seeing that there are two persons in Aphrodite, then there must be two loves too... the first is older and was not generated by any mother. She is the daughter of the Heavens and we call her uranian or celestial Aphrodite. The younger one is the daughter of Zeus and Dione and is called popular or common Aphrodite. It follows, ineluctably, that Love too, being the assistant of the latter, is called popular or common, the other one is called uranian or celestial»[30]

In *Phaedrus* too there is mention of two "impulses" that «rule and lead», one of which guides us towards worldly acquisition, the other «tends towards the good» (237, d). We have just stated that the one is sensible love, the other intelligible and expressed by the Intellect of Love.

Intellect of Love (which was much venerated and splendidly celebrated by the "Fedeli d'Amore" and by Ficino who extolled Platonic Love) embraces an entity's entire vital circumference and, by transfiguring it, raises it up to Heaven.

«I feel that his valor makes me tremble:
... Watch, if you gaze at her
you will see her virtue rise to the heavens»[31]

What we need therefore is to arouse our Intellect of Love, that supra-individual intelligible mind that we all possess, but which in many still lies dormant.

«...you only have, so to speak, to close your eyes and reawaken that new and changed sight that everybody has but few utilize»[32]

The two "impulses" of which Plato speaks do not represent an absolute duality because what is below is simply the "image" of what is above. Sensorial love *imitates* the paradigm or the model of intelligible Love which, once expressed, integrates the former.

Although both are "generation" in Beauty («it is nothing more and nothing less than a delivery into Beauty, for both the body and the soul» *Symposium*, 206 c) the sensorial one is passing, conflicted and gives rise to birth and death, while the other gives life to the expression of Good, which is above and beyond all polar and worldly conditions.

Let us expand the shining flame which burns within our hearts thanks to the spirit of Love-Eros, a flame which raises us up to sweet *Pulchritudo* (Beauty) and which permits us to taste ineffable *Dulcedo* (Sweetness) and experience the inebriating melody of supreme *Beatitudo.*

45. This is the true Science of Love, hermetically handed down to us from the dawn of time, a Science that goes beyond utilitarian and finalized thought («pleasure and usefulness are not Beauty» *Hippias Major* 296 d). It can be grasped through the Intellect of Love, the only means by which to discover the Sacred Mystery.

We now wish to quote a few pages from the great Athenian Master in which he describes the various degrees of Love: from corporeal or sensible beauty to the Idea of Beauty *per se*. Some believe that these are among the most beautiful and elevated pages ever conceived by the human mind.

«To this part of the Teaching of Love, may be you Socrates also could be initiated [the Science of Love is a fact of initiation, it is therefore necessary to bear it in mind]. However there are the *perfect and supreme types of initiation*; there is the ultimate vision. And all this preamble is with a view to that, provided we seek it in the right way. I do not know for sure if you will be capable of this supreme initiation...

Therefore, said she, those who wish to devote themselves, using this method, to the achievement of such an enormous undertaking, must, when still young, *begin* to pursue beauty of mien and body... [The first stage is love of corporeal forms in general].

But then they must consider that Beauty, when it springs from the soul, is far more precious and elevated than that which takes bodily form... [The second stage is that of Love which, rather than towards bodies, turns towards the Souls that dwell in and reveal themselves through them].

Those who have been led, step by step, to these heights of the Science of Love, contemplating all beauty in succession and availing of the proper means, shall arrive *at last* to consummation of the loving Science. And then, by a sudden vision, they shall contemplate something amazingly and objectively beautiful by its very nature.

This is Beauty, the prime reason and aim of all the preceding, painstaking exercises. She always is, she does not become, does not perish, nor does she increase or diminish...

Yet this Beauty must not be thought of as having a face, hands, anything belonging to a body.

Not for sure is she discourse, nor is she cognition... This Beauty by itself, with itself, for itself, in all its pure objectivity, is forever in a sole aspect. On the contrary, the other beautiful things participate in a mysterious way of this sole Beauty. But beautiful things [which belong to the sensible world] are born and perish; Beauty suffers nothing, she does not become greater or smaller for any reason at all...

The proper method to pursue initiation in love, whether alone or led by others, is this: take inspiration from the beautiful things of this earth, but always keep supreme Beauty, which is the ultimate goal, present and continue upward. And it will be like *climbing the steps of an ascending stairway.* From the semblance of one to those of two, from those of two to all bodily semblances informed by beauty; then, from these corporeal semblances to beauty of deed and habit;

and from beauty of deed and habit to beauty
of cognition. From cognition to arrive at last,
as to one's destination, to supreme cognition,
no longer cognition of something extraneous,
but cognition of that Beauty.
And so man reaches his *end*: knows beauty
in all its objectivity; that Beauty which exists
in Being»[33]

«And so man reaches his end: knows
Beauty». For the ancient Greeks to know
is *to be*; but Platonic ascension to Beauty
does not only speak of some unfulfilled
and unfufillable aspiration, but of a destination: the lover must reunite himself with the
Beloved, just as the beautiful must reunite
itself with Beauty because the former is but
the *simulacrum* or semblance of the latter.

«In fact, how could one speak of Him as separate, when, in the act of contemplation, one
who saw Him did not see Him as different,
but saw Him as one with himself?»[34]

NOTES

[1] For the Alchemical phases see: Ch. I, Raphael, *The Threefold Pathway of Fire*. Aurea Vidyā. New York.

[2] Plato, *Phaedrus*, 250 e. In, *Plato, The Dialogues*. Edited by E. Turolla. Rizzoli. Milan. (Italian Edition).

[3] Raphael, *The Threefold Pathway of Fire*: II, 82. Op. cit.

[4] Plato, *Symposium*, 191 d. Op.cit.

[5] Plato, *Politeìa*, 521 c. Op. cit.

[6] *Bhagavadgitā*, II, 69. Translation from the Sanskrit and Commentary by Raphael. Edizioni Āśram Vidyā. Rome. (Italian Edition).

[7] Raphael, *The Threefold Pathway of Fire*, I, II, 21. Op. cit.

[8] Plotinus, *Enneads*, I, 6, IX. In, V. Cilento. *Plotino, Enneadi. Prima versione integra e commentario critico*. Laterza. Bari. Italy. (Italian Edition).

[9] Plato, *Symposium*, 192 e. Op. cit.

[10] For the Orphic Theogony see, Raphael, *Orphism and the Initiatory Tradition*, Aurea Vidyā, New York.

[11] Plato: *Symposium*, 178 b. Op. cit.

[12] Marsilio Ficino. *L'Essenza dell'Amore*. Atanor. Rome. (Italian Edition).

[13] Rollo May, *L'amore e la Volontà*, Astrolabio, Rome. (Italian Edition).

[14] Guido Guinizelli, *Rime*, XXVI.

[15] Guido Cavalcanti, *Natura d'Amore.* XXVI.

[16] Plato, *Philebus*, 64 e – 65a. Op. cit.

[17] Plato, *Symposium*, 178 d. Op. cit.

[18] Plotinus, *Enneads*, VI, 9, IX. Op. cit.

[19] Marsilio Ficino. *L'Essenza dell'Amore.* Op. cit.

[20] Plato, *Symposium*, 178 c-d; 181 a; 206 c. In, *Plato, All the writings.* Edited by G. Reale. Bompiani. Milan. (Italian Edition).

[21] Plato, *Philebus*, 54 d. In, *Plato, The Dialogues.* Op. cit.

[22] Raphael, *The Threefold Pathway of Fire*, I, II,13. Op cit.

[23] Plato, *Phaedrus*, 244 e. In, *Plato, The Dialogues.* Op. cit.

[24] Plotinus, *Enneads*, I, 6, IV. Op. cit.

[25] *Ibid.* VI, 9, XI

[26] *Ibid.* I, 6, IX.

[27] Plato, *Phaedrus*, 250 d. In, *Plato, The Dialogues.* Op. cit.

[28] E. Turolla on Plato's *Symposium.*

[29] Plotinus, *Enneads*, I, 6, VII. Op. cit.

[30] Plato, *Symposium*, 180 c-d-e. In, *Plato, The Dialogues.* Op. cit.

[31] Guido Cavalcanti, *Natura d'Amore.* Op. cit.

[32] Plotinus, *Enneads*, I, 6, VIII. Op. cit.

[33] Plato, *Symposium*, 210 e and fl. In, *Plato, The Dialogues* Op. cit.

[34] Plotinus, *Enneads*, VI, 9, X. Op. cit.

GLOSSARY

Affection: All sentiment, impulse, movement of the psyche felt towards people, things, events. Every feeling which fills the soul with anxiety, pity, hatred, indignation, friendship etc. Therefore, its nature is attractive-repulsive and within the same person one may turn into the other.

Arché (ἀρχή): Archetype, suprasensible "model", principle.

Bhakti: Active and loving participation in the Divine. Ardent devotion for the Divinity.

Cakra: Wheel, circle. Hindu anatomy and physiology recognize seven main *cakra* situated along the spinal cord, which are accumulators and dispensers of *prāṇa* or vital energy. They also correspond to states of consciousness.

Conversion of the Soul: Awakening to the reality of the intelligible, which implies a turning, a complete conversion of consciousness.

Dianoetic mind: The analytical, concrete, ob-
jectifying, empirical mind, which directs its attention towards the sensible world. (See also
Diánoia).

Diánoia: (as in Plato). A degree of knowledge
of the intelligible. It corresponds to reasoned
knowledge, where *nóesis* corresponds to pure in-
tellection. (See also *Dianoetic mind* and *Noetic
mind*).

Eros: Love. According to Orphism it is the
principle which animates the universe. In Plato
it takes on a philosophical and religious meaning and represents the intense aspiration to unite
with the Idea of Good or to become *whole* again
(divine hermaphrodite).

Fedeli d'Amore: (Followers of Love). A
Confraternity in Medieval Italy, of which Dante
himself was part, who corresponded among
themselves, in veiled rhyme and prose, their recognition of the Science of Love.

Filía (φιλία): Platonic Love. *Friendship*.

Gnôsis: See *Jñāna*

Good: For Plato it is the absolute or supreme
Idea from which all things, both intelligible and

sensible, draw nourishment, reality and know-ableness. Good is the ontological and metaphysical basis of all existence. It is God or impersonal Reality which sustains the cosmos, it is the metaphysical Principle or the uncaused Cause. It is beyond Being itself.

Hermetic Tradition: Branch of Traditional Knowledge belonging to Egypt and Greece and founded by Hermes Trismegistus.

Hiraṇyagarbha: The totality of subtle manifestation on the universal order whose corresponding individuated subtle aspect is the *jīva* (soul).

Hyperuranus: This state is beyond formal and non-formal cosmos. It is an a-spatial, a-temporal condition. Therefore it is not a *place* as we normally mean it. According to the ancient classics the cosmos was composed of:

– The sensible, phenomenal world
– The mean or heavenly world
– The world of Pure Ideas
– Hyper-Uranus

These worlds correspond to:

– Sensible world (mere multiplicity)
– Intelligible world (the many forms in the One)
– Divine world (Undivided Unity)

Idea: Supra-sensible Reality, the archetype, the intelligible model. Every sensible and intelligible, particular and universal body-form, must be supported by an archetype, a prime model, a primary example from which all the other body-forms are copied or created, participating in the characteristics of the Idea.

Individuality: The empirical, psychological ego which expresses itself through the physical, emotional and empirical mental bodies. Each being in itself is distinct from all other individuals. Each one follows the law of attraction and repulsion, of pleasure and profit. Individuality, as such, does not correspond to the *whole* of being.

Intelligible: Supra-individual, supra-sensible, beyond the world of names and forms. Universal dimension. The intelligible gives form to intelligence.

Intelligible Beauty : The Idea of Beauty (τὸ καλόν) underlying forms. It is Beauty in itself which is not subject to change and cannot perish. According to Plato and the classical philosophers, Beauty is identical with Love-Eros and therefore with Supreme Good. The beautiful forms of the phenomenal world are simply prototypes, copies (which undergo deterioration) of the Idea of Beauty which is and does not become.

The Idea of Beauty is the metaphysical basis of whatever is beautiful in the world of forms and senses. It is the *constant* underlying all things. The world of forms is but an exterior, changing image-appearance of the Idea.

Intelligible Love: Supra-individual, universal Love which includes and integrates individual love.

Intelligible world: this is the world or sphere of Souls which have abandoned the sensible world of generation, of Souls which have transcended or integrated the individualized condition. The intelligible permeates the sensible, just as the psyche permeates the gross physical. Therefore, these worlds, in all their expressive qualities, may be realized upon the dense physical or gross existential plane. The Idea permeates the entire universe in each of its innumerable shades of expression.

Īśvara: Divine Personality. God-Person. The first Principle which corresponds to the universal causal body and comprehends the subtle and gross levels of manifestation.

Jñāna or *gnôsis*: Knowledge of the Traditional Metaphyisical order. Knowledge of a cathartic and realizative import. Knowledge-consciousness.

Kóra (χώρα): Undifferentiated "matter", the substratum of all forms both at gross and subtle levels.

Madonna: For the "Fedeli d'Amore" is the Sacred Knowledge, the Intellect of Love, which Dante personifies in Beatrice.

Noetic mind: The synthetic, intuitive, supra-conscious mind, pure intellect, the Intellect of Love directed towards the intelligible world.

Noûs (νοῦς): This term is rather vast and contains too many implications to be expressed in a sole concept. We can say, however, that for Plato it meant the Soul standing above its "reflection" which had fallen into the world of generation. It is the "divine eye of the Soul", the supreme order-giving Intelligence.

Personality: Soul, the supra-egoic state. of the being. Personality includes both the individual and the universal states of being. In classical Greece the being was considered to be composed of:

- Pnêuma   =   Spirit
- Psyché   =   Soul
- Sôma   =   Body

Philosophia Perennis: The Perennial Philosophy or Traditional Knowledge not originated by humankind. The Philosophy which has as its object pure Being or Reality in itself beyond all phenomenal becoming. It corresponds to the *Sanātana Dharma* of the East.

Prakṛti: Matter, substance out of which all things are made. (See also *Kóra* and *Puruṣa)*.

Prāṇa: Vital, cosmic "breath", energy at the pure state. The flow of energy which sustains and gives life to dense physical beings. It has also many other meanings.

Psyché (ψυχή): Individual soul, a reflection, or moment-in-consciousness, of the universal Soul;

Puruṣa: Essence as the positive polar principle of manifestation, of which the other pole is represented by *prakṛti*, or substance.

Rasa: Taste, flavour, the ability to perceive a quality.

Sensible: What is perceived through the senses. (See also *Sensible world*).

Sensible Beauty: Refers to the multiple body-forms of the phenomenal world. This kind of beauty creates duality: subject and object.

Sensible Love: Desire of a sensible and subjective kind referring to body-forms.

Sensible world: The phenomenal world of forms, all we perceive through the senses or sensorial apparatus. This is the individual world or sphere.

Sentiment: The faculty which permits us to "feel" psychologically. A movement of the soul towards something. Understanding through the senses. Sensorial impression. The range of feelings begins with emotions, develops through sentiment to arrive, quite often, at passion. Subjective movement of the soul.

Sentimentalism: Degeneration of sentiment. There are ethical, aesthetic, intellectual, religious sentiments, etc. Also perceptive sensitivity in general. A vague psychic characteristic which expresses pleasure or pain as distinct from aspects of the intellect and the will. It is often synonymous with affection.

Sôma (σῶμα): The dense physical body.

Soul: The ontological ego, inclusive awareness, the Self, the Noûs, a reflection of which enters the world of the senses.

Summum Bonum: The Supreme Good. The platonic One-Good, the One of Plotinus. Absolute.

The Threefold Pathway of Fire. A work by Raphael where three ways or paths of Realization are explained: Alchemy, Love of Beauty, Traditional Metaphysics.

Tradition: "That which is transmitted". The Perennial Law or *Lex Perennis*, not originated by humankind, which sets the rules for a cycle of manifestation. Knowledge, set of revealed Scriptures which include the Traditional Knowledge. *sôma*

Traditional or *Initiatory Metaphysics*: Knowledge handed down through the ages but not of a human order. Spiritual or divine Knowledge. *Philosophia Perennis*. The Hindus designate this kind of traditional Doctrine by the term *Sanātana Dharma*. *Sanātana* denotes the perennial nature and the perpetuity of a Doctrine which remains constant through a whole *manvantara* (cosmic cycle). The word *dharma* in this context means "in conformity with the Order"; it is the constant and unchanging direction of the universal Order which permeates or forms the basis of the entire manifestation. It is the Pole around which all contingencies and all sensible knowledge rotate. Thus the Philosophy we speak of in the text is not the limited and systematic conception of a single individual considered exclusively in its human dimension

Vedānta: (Literally, "end of the *Veda*" both as final part and purpose). Branch of the Eastern Tradition based mainly on the teaching of the *Upaniṣad*. It may also mean *"Upaniṣad"* because these form the concluding part of the *Veda*.

Vidyā: Knowledge of the Metaphysical Reality

Virāṭ: The totality of the gross manfestation.

Yoga: "Union". Traditional Doctrine that proposes the unity of Life. Method to realize this union.

INDEX

A

accord 20, 25, 116
Accord 25, 57, 58, 60, 63
affection 28, 80, 142
Affection **135***
ājñā 77, 79, 81, 82
Ājñā 75
ākāśa 88, 89
Alchemy 18, 144
anāhata 77, 80
Anāhata 75
aparavidyā 30
ἀρχή 135
Arché **135**
Archetype 59
Art 94
a-spatial 137
a-temporal 137
attraction-repulsion 28

* Page numbers in bold type refer to a Glossary entry.

B

bīja 80
Beatrice 32, 102, 104, 140
beautiful 44, 108, 110, 115, 117, 119, 121, 123,
    128, 130, 131, 138, 139
Beautiful 61, 110, 116
beauty 62, 106, 107, 108, 109, 110, 115, 116, 117,
    118, 119, 120, 123, 125, 128, 129, 130, 131,
    142
Beauty 9, 15, 44, 48, 50, 61, 63, 66, 94, 101, 104,
    105, 107, 108, 110, 113, 115, 117, 118, 119,
    121, 122, 123, 125, 127, 128, 129, 130, 131,
    138, 142, 144
beloved 83, 104, 108
Beloved 49, 109, 131
Bhagavadgītā 52
bhakti 30, 105
Bhakti 105, **135**
Binah 18
Bodies 36
body 12, 13, 19, 20, 25, 29, 30, 31, 67, 73, 75, 79,
    100, 109, 111, 119, 124, 127, 129, 130, 138,
    142
Body 33, 35, 74, 140
body-form 79, 138, 142
body-forms 100, 138, 142
Book of the Dead 88

C

cakra 9, 75, 77, 79, 80, 81, 82, 83, 135
Cakra **135**
Canticle of Canticles 83, 104

causal body 19
Cháos 87, 88, 89, 90
Chokmah 18
consciousness 33, 35, 47, 48, 53, 67, 135
constant 117, 139, 143
contemplation 48, 66, 109, 116, 118, 119, 120, 123,
    131
Contemplation 103, 119
conversion 52
conversion of the Soul 52
Conversion of the Soul **134**
cosmos 87, 137
creator 90
Creator 11
Creature 11

D

Dante 7, 102, 103, 104, 134, 140
desire 5, 28, 38, 43, 44, 48, 53, 54, 55, 56, 57, 58,
    65, 80, 93, 94, 103, 109, 120, 121, 124
Desire 28, 54, 56
dianoetic 105, 119
Dianoetic 135, 136
Dianoetic Mind **135**
Diánoia **136**
duality 17, 18, 28, 50, 55, 68, 109, 120, 122, 127,
    142

E

ego 29, 36, 37, 38, 47, 53, 54, 55, 60, 81, 124, 138,
    143
Ego 36, 124

emotion 11, 29, 59, 74, 115
emotional body 20
Emotional body 124
entity 9, 30, 36, 37, 55, 59, 77, 101, 109, 115, 119,
    122, 126
Eros 9, 50, 51, 85, 87, 89, 90, 91, 92, 93, 94, 95, 97,
    99, 100, 101, 105, 106, 111, 121, 122, 128,
    136, 138
essence 18, 20, 55, 100, 101, 109, 122, 123

F

Fedeli d'Amore 83, 101, 102, 103, 126, **136**, 140
feeling 28, 29, 30, 115, 118, 121, 135
Feeling 28
φιλία 28, **136**
filía 28
Filía **136**
fire 22, 80, 89, 107
Fire 15, 33, 63, 71, 77, 89, 92, 113, 122, 133, 134,
    144
focal Point 45
Friendship 136
fullness 55
Fullness 55

G

gnôsis 30, **139**
good 18, 22, 28, 52, 108, 125, 126
Good 51, 94, 106, 110, 128, **136**, 138, 143
gross plane 19

H

harmony 20, 48, 57, 58, 120
Harmony 27, 57, 60, 63, 105
heart 40, 49, 54, 77, 80, 81, 93, 102, 103, 106
Heart 15, 53, 75
heat 66, 70, 92
Hermes Trismegistus 137
hermetic Tradition 35
Hermetic Tradition **137**
Hiraṇyagarbha 19, 88, **137**
Hyperuranus 107, **137**

I

idea 29, 94, 103, 115
Idea 66, 106, 109, 110, 116, 117, 118, 119, 122,
    125, 128, 136, **138**
image 127, 139
immortal 49, 60
incomplete 31, 37, 100, 124
individual 13, 28, 31, 43, 46, 51, 53, 66, 71, 73, 74,
    82, 127, 138, 139, 140, 142, 144
individuality 37, 38, 55
Individuality **138**
initiated Poet 48
Initiatory Metaphysics **144**
instinct 26, 38, 44, 45, 48, 59, 93
instincts 26, 43
intellect 29, 81, 140, 142
Intellect 5, 29, 59, 60, 66, 81, 83, 102, 124, 126,
    128, 140
Intellect of Love 5, 29, 59, 60, 66, 81, 83, 102, 124,
    126, 128, 140

149

intelligible 48, 67, 87, 88, 89, 100, 101, 106, 108,
      109, 116, 119, 122, 124, 125, 126, 136, 138,
      139, 140
Intelligible 124, 137, **138, 139**
Īśvara 19, **139**

J

jñāna 30, 91
Jñāna 136, **139**

K

καλόν 106, 138
knowledge 12, 30, 51, 54, 91, 119, 143
Knowledge 13, 30, 50, 88, 91, 94, 110, 137, 140,
      141, 143
kóra 88, 100
Kóra **140**, 141
Kuṇḍalinī 79

L

light 48, 66, 92, 96, 103, 104, 112
love 11, 12, 22, 40, 43, 44, 45, 48, 51, 54, 56, 58,
      92, 101, 103, 104, 107, 109, 110, 115, 117,
      121, 123, 124, 125, 126, 127, 129, 130, 139
Love 5, 7, 9, 11, 12, 13, 23, 29, 31, 36, 38, 41, 43,
      44, 45, 47, 48, 49, 50, 51, 52, 53, 54, 55, 56,
      57, 58, 59, 60, 63, 66, 67, 79, 81, 82, 83, 89,
      90, 91, 92, 93, 94, 101, 102, 103, 105, 106,
      107, 108, 109, 110, 113, 116, 120, 122, 123,
      125, 127, 128, 129, 136, 138, 139, 140, 142,
      144

150

M

mūlādhāra 79, 80
Mūlādhāra 75
Madonna 48, 54, 102, **140**
maṇipura 77, 80, 81
Maṇipura 75
mental body 20, 73
Mental body 124
Mercury 18, 35, 36
mind 31, 35, 45, 53, 56, 59, 80, 81, 82, 92, 93, 127,
     128, 135, 140
Mind 48
multiplicity 50, 110
mysteries 118
Mysteries 104
myth 87, 88, 121
Myth 50, 89, 91

N

noetic 20, 25, 35, 100, 101
Noetic 36, 74, 136, **140**
νοῦς **140**
Noûs 101, 110, **140**

O

one 13, 19, 20, 23, 29, 30, 32, 38, 40, 49, 50, 51, 57,
     66, 70, 71, 73, 74, 76, 82, 85, 101, 105, 108,
     109, 110, 111, 115, 116, 117, 118, 120, 123,
     124, 126, 127, 130, 131, 135, 138
One 19, 50, 93, 94, 121, 143
ontological 93, 94, 124, 136, 143

151

Ontological 124
opus 35, 50
Orphism 87, 133, 136
ουσία 100

P

Paradiso 7, 14, 22, 32, 40, 62, 70, 76, 84, 96, 112,
    134
paravidyā 30
pax profunda 51
person 12, 28, 115, 135
Person 56
Personality 36, **140**
Philosophia 35, 51, 141, 143
Philosophia Perennis 35, **141**, 143
Philosophical Love 11, 13
physical body 20, 73, 75
Physical body 124
plane 17, 18, 19, 37, 50, 51, 65, 66, 87, 100, 106,
    139
planes of existence 17, 19
Plato 23, 28, 41, 51, 57, 82, 83, 88, 94, 97, 99, 100,
    101, 102, 103, 104, 107, 109, 115, 123, 127,
    134, 136, 138, 140
Platonic 9, 126, 131
pnêuma 35
Pnêuma 140
poet 90
Poet 48
point 13, 17, 18, 27, 31, 44, 57, 59, 60, 74, 92, 93,
    102, 108
Point 45

polar 12, 26, 45, 48, 57, 58, 65, 67, 74, 92, 128
Polar 9
polarities 17, 20, 74, 75, 82
Polarities 9
polarity 9, 11, 17, 18, 19, 20, 27, 28, 29, 30, 57, 68, 73, 74, 81, 82, 83
Polarity 17, 71, 74
prāṇa 75, 135
Prāṇa 141
prakṛti 18, 27, 88, 101, 141
Prakṛti **141**
principle 18, 89, 117, 136
Principle 13, 59, 91, 119, 137
principles 29, 67, 82, 87, 93, 116
proportion 106
proportions 57
psyche 12, 13, 31, 53, 135, 139
psyché 35, 101
Psyché 106, 140, **141**
puruṣa 18, 27
Puruṣa **141**

Q

qualities 26, 30, 31, 73, 139
quality 59, 115, 141

R

Rasa **141**
reflection 54, 100, 101, 117, 118, 125, 140, 143
reflections 108

S

sacred 19, 41, 48, 49, 89
sahasrāra 82
Sahasrāra 75
Salt 35
Sanātana Dharma 141, 143
science 23, 29
Science 5, 23, 31, 79, 94, 101, 103, 104, 105, 128,
      129
Science of Love 5, 23, 31, 79, 94, 101, 103, 104,
      105, 128, 129
sensible 88, 100, 101, 107, 115, 117, 118, 119, 123,
      125, 126, 128, 130, 136, 138, 139, 142
Sensible 115, 124, 137, **141, 142**
sentiment 11, 59, 105, 135, 142, 143
Sentiment **142**
Sentimentalism **142**
sephirotic Tree 18
sex 11, 12, 26, 27, 45, 46, 47, 50, 65, 73, 94
sexual 12, 26, 27, 43, 44, 45, 46, 48, 77, 79, 80, 116
Sexual 27
sexuality 13, 44, 45, 46
silence 60, 87
σῶμα **142**
sôma 35
Sôma 140, **142**
soul 12, 28, 44, 45, 59, 61, 84, 93, 103, 111, 118,
      121, 127, 129, 135, 137, 141, 142
Soul 12, 13, 33, 35, 52, 55, 56, 81, 83, 90, 94, 100,
      101, 106, 107, 108, 109, 110, 117, 118, 122,
      124, 125, 140, 141, **143**

154

sphere 12, 13, 30, 107, 139, 142
spirit 57, 77, 120, 128
Spirit 33, 35, 140
substance 18, 20, 101, 122
subtle 19, 75, 87
subtle plane 19
Sulphur 18, 35, 36
Summum Bonum **143**
supra-individual 13, 127, 138, 139
supreme knowledge 30
svādhiṣṭhāṇa 77, 79, 81
Svādhiṣṭhāṇa 75

T

Theogony 101, 133
The Threefold Pathway of Fire **143**
τὸ καλόν 106, 138
Tradition 20, 35, 91, 103, 133, 137, **143**
traditional Knowledge 88
Traditional Knowledge 94, 137, 141, 143
Traditional Metaphysics **143**
truth 50, 106, 112

U

unity 17, 33, 52, 56, 59, 91, 92, 93, 144
Unity 9, 17, 33, 52, 137
universal 18, 19, 29, 30, 37, 48, 60, 82, 88, 109,
        121, 138, 139, 140, 143
Universal 13, 67, 74, 116, 138
Upaniṣad 144

V

Veda 144
Vedānta 18, 19, 88, 91, 101, **144**
vibration 18, 57, 59, 60, 67, 117
Vidyā 3, 4, 5, 133, **144**
Virāṭ 19, **144**
vision 84, 104, 120, 122, 129
Vision 19, 60, 108
viśuddha 77, 80, 81
Viśuddha 75

χ

χώρα 88, 100, 101, **140**

W

whole 19, 33, 37, 38, 47, 50, 51, 83, 94, 96, 100,
        106, 110, 136, 138, 143
Whole 37, 51, 82
Wisdom 50, 53, 67, 92, 101, 102, 104, 105, 123

Ψ

ψυχή 52, **141**
ψυχή περιαγογή 52

Y

Yoga 75, **144**

Z

Zend Avesta 89

RAPHAEL
Unity of Tradition

Raphael, having attained a synthesis of Knowledge (which is not to be associated with eclecticism or with syncretism), aims at "presenting" the Universal Tradition in its many Eastern and Western expressions. He has spent a substantial number of years writing and publishing books on the spiritual experience; his works include commentaries on the *Qabbālāh*, Hermeticism and Alchemy. He has also commented on and compared the Orphic Tradition with the works of Plato, Parmenides and Plotinus. Furthermore, Raphael is the author of several books on the pathway of non-duality (*Advaita*), which he has translated from the original Sanskrit, offering commentaries on a number of key Vedāntic texts.

With reference to Platonism, Raphael has highlighted the fact that if we were to draw a parallel between Śaṅkara's *Advaita Vedānta* and a Traditional Western Philosophical Vision we could refer to the Vision presented by Plato. Drawing such a parallel does not imply a search for reciprocal influences, but rather it points to something of paramount importance: a sole Truth, inherent in the doctrines (teachings) of several great thinkers, who although far apart in time and space, have reached similar and in some cases even identical conclusions.

One notices how Raphael's writings aim to manifest and underscore the Unity of Tradition, under the metaphysical perspective. This does not mean that he is in opposition to the dualistic perspective, or to the various religious faiths, or "points of view".

An embodied real metaphysical Vision cannot be opposed to anything. What counts for Raphael is the unveiling, through living and being, of that level of Truth which one has been able to contemplate.

In the light of the Unity of Tradition, Raphael's writings and commentaries offer to the intuition of the reader, precise points of correspondence between Eastern and Western Teachings. These points of reference are useful for those who want to address a comparative Doctrinal study and to enter the spirit of the Unity of Teaching.

For those who follow either the Eastern or the Western traditional line these correspondences help in comprehending how the *Philosophia Perennis* (Universal Tradition), which has no history and has not been formulated by human minds as such, «comprehends universal truths that do not belong to any people or any age». It is only for lack of "comprehension" or of "synthetic vision" that one particular Branch is considered the only reliable one. From this position there can be but opposition and fanaticism. What degenerates the Doctrine is sentimental, fanatical devotionalism as well as proud intellectualism, which is critical and sterile, dogmatic and separative.

In Raphael's words: «For those of us who aim at Realization, it is our task to get to the essence of every Doctrine, because we know that as Truth is one, so Tradition is one even if, just like Truth, Tradition may be viewed from a plurality of apparently different points of view. We must abandon all disquisitions concerning the phenomenal process of becoming, and move onto the plane of Being. In other words: we must have a Philosophy of Being as the foundation of our search and of our realization»[1].

Raphael interprets spiritual practice as a "Path of Fire". Here is what he writes: «... The "Path of Fire" is the pathway each disciple follows in all branches of Tradition; it is the Way of Return. Therefore, it is not the particular teaching of an individual, nor a path parallel to the one and only Main Road... After all, every disciple follows his own "Path of Fire", no matter which Branch of Tradition he belongs to».

[1] See, Raphael, *Tat tvam asi*, That thou art. Aurea Vidyā. New York.

In Raphael's view, what is important is to express through living and being the truth that one has been able to contemplate. Thus, for each being, the expression of thought and action must be coherent and in agreement with one's own and specific *dharma*.

After more than thirty-five years of teaching, both oral and written, Raphael is now dedicating himself only to those people who wish to be "doers" rather than "sayers", according to St. Paul's expression.

Raphael is connected with the *maṭha* founded by Śrī Ādi Śaṅkara at Śṛṅgeri and Kāñcīpuram as well as with the Rāmaṇa Āśram at Tiruvannamalai.

Founder of the Āśram Vidyā Order, he now dedicates himself entirely to the spiritual practice. He lives in a hermitage connected to the *āśram* and devotes himself completely to a vow of silence.

* * *

May Raphael's Consciousness, expression of Unity of Tradition, guide and illumine along this Opus all those who donate their *mens informalis* (non-formal mind) to the attainment of the highest known Realization.

PUBLICATIONS

Books by Raphael
published in English

At the Source of Life
Aurea Vidyā, New York

Beyond the illusion of the ego
Aurea Vidyā, New York

Essence and Purpose of Yoga
The Initiatory Pathways to the Transcendent
Element Books, Shaftesbury, U.K.

Initiation into the Philosophy of Plato
Aurea Vidyā, New York

Orphism and the Initiatory Tradition
Aurea Vidyā, New York

Pathway of Fire, Initiation to the Kabbalah
S. Weiser, York Beach, Maine, U.S.A.

The Pathway of Non-duality, Advaitavāda
Motilal Banarsidass, New Delhi

Tat tvam asi, That thou art,
The Path of Fire According to the Aspar5avāda
Aurea Vidyā, New York

The Threefold Pathway of Fire
Aurea Vidyā, New York

Traditional Classics
in English

Śaṅkara, *Ātmabodha**,
Self-knowledge.
Aurea Vidyā , New York

Śaṅkara, *Drigdriśyaviveka**,
Discernment between *ātman* and non-*ātman*.
Aurea Vidyā, New York

Gauḍapāda, *Māṇḍūkyakārikā**,
The Māṇḍūkya Upaniṣad with the verses-*kārikā* of
Gauḍapāda and Commentary by Raphael.
Aurea Vidyā, New York

Parmenides, *On the Order of Nature*, Περί
φύσεως**,
For a Philosophical Ascesis.
Aurea Vidyā, New York

166

Śaṅkara, *Vivekacūḍāmaṇi**,
The Crest-jewel of Discernment.
Aurea Vidyā, New York

Forthcoming Publications
in English

Patañjali, *The Regal Way to Realization**,
Yogadarśana

Śaṅkara, *Aparokṣānubhūti**, Self-realization

Raphael, *Fire of Awakening*

The Bhagavadgītā*

Bādarāyaṇa, *Brahmasūtra**

Five Upaniṣads*, Īśa, Kaivalya, Sarvasāra,
Amṛtabindu, Atharvaśiran

Raphael, *Which Democracy?*

* Translated from the Sanskrit, and Commented, by
Raphael
** Edited by Raphael

Aurea Vidyā is the Publishing House of the Parmenides Traditional Philosophy Foundation, a Not-for-Profit Organization whose purpose is to make Perennial Philosophy accessible.

The Foundation goes about its purpose in a number of ways: by publishing and distributing Traditional Philosophy texts with Aurea Vidyā, by offering individual and group encounters and by providing a Reading Room and daily Meditations at its Center.

* * *

Those readers who have an interest in Traditional Philosophy are welcome to contact the Foundation at the address shown on the colophon page.

Lightning Source UK Ltd.
Milton Keynes UK
UKHW011227011121
393193UK00002B/714

9 781931 406123